SPEEDQUEST!
INSIDE THE BLUE FLAME

The Inside Story of how *The Blue Flame* became the last
American car to hold the World Land Speed Record

Richard Keller

David Tremayne

Intellect Publishing, LLC

DO NOT CITE IN ANY CONTEXT

WITHOUT PERMISSION OF THE AUTHORS

V-9

Copyright©2020 Richard A Keller

ISBN: 978-1-945190-95-7

To contact the authors:

Richard A. Keller, III,

dickkeller630@gmail.com.

David Tremayne,

restspirit@aol.com

www. IntellectPublishing.com

AUTHOR'S NOTE

I began writing this story early in the 1970s. Most of my author contribution is written in the first person.

In 2010 I was assisted by David Tremayne in completing this document. David is a UK based motor racing journalist. He has written extensively about the Land Speed Record over the past three decades in several books and is the Formula One correspondent for *The Independent*, a British news publisher.

David made several suggestions that helped in writing my accounts in this book. When it came to interviewing other teammates and participants in telling *The Blue Flame* story, I asked David to write those chapters in order to keep my opinions out of their stories. His authorship will be found in chapters 6, 7, 8, 9, 10, and 13.

For his excellent work I am extremely grateful.

Richard Keller

2020

RICHARD KELLER & DAVID TREMAYNE

CONTENTS

DEDICATION

This publication is dedicated to my grandchildren: Kaley Elizabeth Weichert; Heidi Alyse Weichert; Eli James Weichert; Aurelien Timothy Jacques Keller; Guillaume Charles Tam Minh Keller; Simon Peter Keller; Jack Whitman Keller; Hazel Keller; great-grandson Khiry James Foster; and those to be named later.

And also to my great departed friend Charles Manford Suba, speed demon, and co-conspirator. He left us October 13, 1968, way too early.

RICHARD KELLER & DAVID TREMAYNE

FOREWORD

by

DAVID TREMAYNE

I remember when I was a teenager the feelings that my first sight of photographs of *The Blue Flame* aroused in me.

Already a disciple of the land speed record all those years back, I thought it was on a par with the *Golden Arrow* and *Goldenrod*, arguably the most beautiful car ever to attempt the record. I still feel that way. I remember touching the car, talking to it, the first time I saw it in the metal, at the Auto & Technik Museum in Sinsheim which I visited during a German Grand Prix weekend in the Nineties.

How, back in 1981, I had seriously wondered what my chances were of raising £5000 when I heard rumors that it was for sale for that sum in Holland.

I've studied the land speed record since I was 12 years old, written articles and books about it all my professional life, and met a lot of the people who attempted it. And I've been privileged in my life to be present twice when it was broken.

The first time was when Richard Noble took *Thrust2* to 633.468 mph on Black Rock Desert on October 4, 1983, breaking the mile record Gary Gabelich achieved with the Flame. The second when Andy Green did 763.035 mph on October 15, 1997, to become the only man to pierce the sound barrier.

For me, *The Blue Flame* program was one of the greatest record challenges of them all. And here's why.

Back in 1960 five men attempted to break John Cobb's long-standing 394.20 mph record, which dated back to 1947. In The Great Confrontation at Bonneville that August, David was represented by Americans Athol Graham, an impecunious garage mechanic from Salt Lake City with his homebuilt City of Salt Lake; hot rod genius Mickey Thompson and his fiendishly clever *Challenger*; Art Arfons, with his curious *Anteater*; and Doc Nathan Ostich with his ground-breaking pure-thrust *Flying Caduceus*. Against them stood Goliath, in the form of Donald Campbell and his *Bluebird CN7* which had been heavily sponsored by British industry.

None of them succeeded.

Graham was killed. Campbell was lucky to survive a crash at 320 mph. Ostich and Arfons went home realizing their cars weren't yet man enough for the job. Thompson went 406.6 mph one way, only to suffer mechanical misfortune on his return run.

As the speeds had risen beyond 400 mph, it had become very rare for somebody to break the record at their first try.

Tom Green did it with Walt Arfons's *Wingfoot Express* in October 1964 (though the car had been tested elsewhere the previous year), but held the record at 413.20 mph for only three days before Walt's estranged younger brother Art similarly succeeded first time out with his *Green Monster*, at 434.02 mph. That triggered the game of high-speed Russian Roulette in which Arfons and rival Craig Breedlove dueled towards 600 mph that Fall and the next. Breedlove had failed at his first try, at Bonneville in 1962 with his tricycle *Spirit of America*, but come back successfully in 1963 and again in 1964. In 1965 his new *Spirit of America – Sonic 1* also broke the record first time out, at 555.483 mph.

But, without wishing in any way to belittle these fabulous attempts, it's fair to say that Arfons and Breedlove were working in a region that offered abundant potential. The jet car was at an early stage of its development and there was huge potential to raise Cobb's record which had been set in a Railton Special which relied on piston engine power driving through all four wheels. Arfons and Breedlove were in the vanguard of jet car development, literally being pushed along by copious thrust that had no need to rely on traction from the wheels. They proceeded in stages as they felt out their cars, initially using only bursts of afterburner as they explored the limits with incremental speed increases. Both were far more concerned with chassis performance and aerodynamics than they were the behavior of their military surplus turbojet engines, the performance and reliability of which could virtually be taken for granted. These were tried and tested units which used long-established technology.

But *The Blue Flame…*

This was something totally new, for nobody had tried the liquid-fuelled rocket engine before. The pencil-slim monocoque chassis also broke new ground, and only Walt Arfons had essayed the tri-cycle configuration, with the solid-fuel rocket-powered 1965 *Wingfoot Express II*. And Breedlove and Arfons had raised the bar as they maxed out their jet cars at 600 mph.

And the Reaction Dynamics boys had their problems. Oh, boy, did they have their problems! Unlike Green, Breedlove and Arfons, they had less potential for increasing the record and could not take for granted their engine technology, for the rocket powerplant was a whole new ballgame. It under-performed and proved unreliable as they developed it. By contrast, however, their chassis and aerodynamics technology was absolutely spot-on from Day One, a rarity in the land speed field that would prove a major advantage when things finally came together. Then crew morale became stretched with the continual setbacks, and the pressure of expectation from the sponsoring gas industry was ratcheted up with each new delay. The money was running short, and the weather was closing in too. Snow threatened.

In the last hour of what turned out to be their last usable day, *The Blue Flame* team finally broke through with the kilometer record of 630.388 mph and the mile record of 622.407 mph. These were significant increases that showcased the credibility of their achievement. It was already beginning to rain when Gary Gabelich made his return run. The snow came that night.

But they had succeeded. Despite all the setbacks, despite the problems with the dramatic new engine technology, despite the shortage of funds, track and weather as the big moment approached, the Reaction Dynamics crew took home the honors they had gone to Bonneville to win.

At the first attempt.

It was one of the most audacious and impressive efforts in history, and this is its inside story. In some places you'll read of shortcomings, of tensions within the team, sometimes of mistakes that were made. But they weren't unique to *The Blue Flame* program. All record attempts go through similar things, and they aren't to be regarded in a derogatory sense, but rather as necessary steps that all challengers have to take. Sometimes they go the wrong way while finding the right way. That's part and parcel of record breaking, of being pioneers who go to places where nobody else has yet been. It's the sort of mis-stepping you have to go through in order to get on the right track. And the fact that a team might have gone that route is testimony to its inherent strength rather than to any weakness, because adversity only makes the right kind of people stronger, and bonds them closer together. Sometimes it's important to learn how to lose before you learn how to win, and the people who don't get that are those who never get land speed record breaking. Or any other kind of endeavor where you put yourself, either personally or as a collective entity, on the line.

The Blue Flame team put itself on the line many times, right from the moment that Ray Dausman, Pete Farnsworth and Dick Keller set themselves beyond ordinary men and started to do something about their remarkable dream. And for six brutal weeks in September and October 1970 they put themselves under the glare of white salt and media scrutiny in the most unforgiving public arena.

What they achieved there went into the history books. Their mile record of 622.407 mph lasted until October 4th 1983. Their kilometer record of 630.388 mph lasted until September 25th 1997. And people thought John Cobb's final record of 1947 had defined longevity!

There could be no greater testimony to the fact that they not only succeeded, but succeeded brilliantly. All these years later, *The Blue Flame* is still the only rocket-powered car ever to hold the land speed record. And, from the ecological point of view that matters so much more now than it did four decades ago, it is still far and away the most environmentally friendly...

David Tremayne

Darlington, England, December 2011

RICHARD KELLER & DAVID TREMAYNE

INTRODUCTION

October 23, 1970 – Roaring northward across the stark white salt desert The Blue Flame's powerful rocket motor suddenly goes silent; then, it coasts, whistling as it slices through the chilled October air for another three seconds toward the timing lights, standing like tiny black sentinels, at the end of the mile.

KAPOW! The red parachute slams open, abruptly dragging the land missile down from its insane speed so the wheel brakes can finish the job. The Reaction Dynamics crew quickly arrives and unfastens the cockpit canopy while a station wagon, horn blaring and headlights flashing, pulls to a stop with the USAC timing crew and a few reporters in tow.

Chuck Suba photo in Gary's pocket

As driver Gary Gabelich excitedly throws off his helmet, unbuckles his harness, and climbs from the now dormant race car, chief timer Joe Petrali walks hurriedly toward him with the triumphant news. A new World Land Speed Record has been set, 630.388 mph in the kilometer!

Gary's dad, Mehl, runs up and gives him a bear-like hug of joy and relief. With tears in his eyes, Gary turns toward the

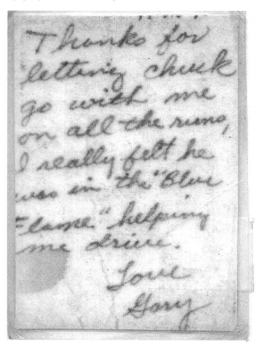

newsmen, smiling, and exclaims quietly: "Listen, I want to dedicate this record to Chuck Suba and his family, because he was supposed to be here to drive the Flame."

In 1997, RAF Wing Commander Andy Green drove Richard Noble's *Thrust SSC* twin-turbojet-powered land speed record vehicle to the first supersonic FIA World Land Speed Record in history. At the same time, he finally broke *The Blue Flame*'s kilometer FIA World Record that had stood for a remarkable 27 years. *Thrust SSC* was an outstanding example of British national pride in technical excellence and sporting competition, its stellar achievement rightly celebrated internationally.

Endorsed rear of Chuck Suba photo

But what is known of the prior World Record holder, *The Blue Flame*, and the technology in its creation? Much like comparing the Formula 1 driving skills of Nuvolari with Fangio, Fangio with Senna, or Senna with Schumacher, these were different times and circumstances. An exploration of that earlier time and those experiences may give an indication of record performances yet to come.

As *Thrust SSC*'s supersonic record was the culmination of the driven compulsion of a single person, Britain's Richard Noble; *The Blue Flame's* records resulted from the consuming quest of three young Americans, in their twenties, who were a product of their times. However, in both cases, a strong supportive cast of individuals and institutions made it a reality (See Tables 1, 2 and 3).

RICHARD KELLER & DAVID TREMAYNE

PROLOGUE

First, let's look at the strategies for setting a record speed on land with a rocket-powered automobile. Federation Internationale de l'Automobile (FIA) proclaims the World Land Speed Record (LSR) to be the fastest FIA World Record regardless of classification. *[Note: per the FIA International Sporting Code – A World Record is a record recognized by the FIA as the best result obtained (for a recognized distance) with a vehicle, not taking the category, group or class of the car into account, provided the car belongs to the types eligible for an attempt at a national or international record. FIA Category C (Special Vehicles) includes the Group: Thrust; Classes: Jet and Rocket.]*

Setting a flying start speed record requires the vehicle to make two timed runs in opposite directions over the measured distance within one hour. At the time we were running, establishing a new land speed record required exceeding an existing record speed by more than 1%.

Distance/Time = Speed

Time. While the LSR is expressed in terms of speed (mph/kph) record setting is really about time. Millisecond timers provide the crucial measurements made by activating photoelectric cells placed at the beginning and end of the measured distance (mile/kilometer). The vehicle breaking a light beam entering the measured distance records the time, then breaking a second light beam exiting that measured distance records a second time. The difference is the elapsed time for that distance. The average of the two elapsed times for the round trip is used to calculate the official average speed for the measured distance.

Note that while only four significant digits of elapsed time are available for the mile or kilometer at high speeds (e.g., 3.543s in the kilometer), the official average speed is calculated to the third decimal, or six digits (e.g., 631.367 mph).

While traversing a mile in six seconds, for example, may sound rather abstract to a layperson, a speed of 600 mph gives everyone a vivid impression of the achievement.

Another important time to record is breaking the final light beam on the returning (second) record run. That must be accomplished within an hour of breaking the first light beam to comply with the FIA regulations for setting records.

Distance:

The shortest distances (and fastest speeds) for FIA-recognized flying start records are the kilometer and the mile. Beginning in the late 19th century, shortly after the arrival of the automobile, land speed records were being set in France over one kilometer distance. France is on the metric system, naturally. Later land speed records set in England and the United States were timed over one mile. Finally, in the Twenties, world records were being set simultaneously over both distances.

At Bonneville, the International Course was a 10 mile straight, flat road surface of scraped hard white salt with a black center line as a reference for the driver. The prepared course surface was 120 ft wide. Time was measured between mile markers five and six providing four or five miles to build up speed (depending upon the direction of travel) before the timing lights, or to stop the vehicle after leaving the timing zone. The kilometer timing trap was offset to one end of the mile, beginning at the six-mile marker and ending 3280.4 ft later. For example when driving south, the first light beam is placed at the start of both the six mile marker (5280 ft) and the kilometer (3,280.4 ft) measured distance. The second light beam is, of course, placed at the kilometer measured distance and the third light beam at the end of the mile. On the return north run, the first light beam begins the timing at the five-mile marker, the second light beam (1,999.6 ft away) begins timing the kilometer and the third light beam completes the timing for both.

Speed:

A rocket motor is operated most efficiently at full power (thrust), so the vehicle will, as a result, continually accelerate until aerodynamic and rolling drag equals the thrust, or propelling force. The fuel supply is finite and the rocket's appetite for it is voracious. Therefore, optimum performance will result from continuous acceleration at full power for the duration of the record attempt. *The Blue Flame* was restricted by agreement with Goodyear Tire Company to not exceed 700 mph in 1970. Rather than accelerate through the full measured distances, maximum average speed would be attained by reaching a peak speed at the mid-point of the measured distance and coasting the remainder (a 700 mph peak speed, for example, would yield a record average speed of approximately 650 mph). This, of course, assumes the acceleration prior to 'burnout' is equal to the deceleration due to (primarily) aerodynamic drag after thrust ceases. In practice this proved reasonably accurate.

Take as an example *The Blue Flame's* fastest runs. On the south run the 1,999.6 ft long trap, after the kilometer, saw a speed of 596 mph, while the kilometer speed was 631. On the north run the 1,999.6 ft long trap, before the kilometer, saw a speed of 624 mph, and the kilometer speed was 629. The maximum speed reached briefly during the record runs on October 23, 1970, at mid-mile, was observed to be 660 mph with onboard instrumentation.

Now, let the story begin!

SPEEDQUEST!

INSIDE THE BLUE FLAME

The Inside Story of how *The Blue Flame* became the last
American car to hold the World Land Speed Record

-1-

REACTION DYNAMICS AND THE ROCKET REVOLUTION

Having been a voracious reader from childhood, my interests followed the many heroic figures that I admired. In the beginning, adventurers and explorers such as Daniel Boone, Davy Crockett, and Kit Carson were rugged achievers who captured my attention. Later, I was fascinated by the determination to succeed of Abraham Lincoln, Thomas Edison, the Wright brothers, and Henry Ford. Later still, I was inspired by reading the daring exploits of race car drivers: Jimmy Murphy, Frank Lockhart, and Wilbur Shaw driving the thundering AAA National Championship cars at Indianapolis, which was not far from my Chicago home, and Tazio Nuvolari, Bernd Rosemeyer, Richard Seaman, and Rudolf Caracciola in European Grand Prix racing.

Exciting advances in aviation following World War II had me looking upward instead of ahead; first the jets, then the space race and powerful rockets. Astronauts were my new heroes whose achievements I supported as an experimental engineer at IIT Research Institute (IITRI), working on NASA-funded projects. My day job involved developing defensive countermeasures for military space satellites, real-time monitoring of rocket fuelling for the Saturn I and Saturn V boosters for Project Apollo, and stable thermal coatings for communications satellites. Being practical, hotrodding and drag racing would have to serve to satisfy my earthbound growing appetite for technology and speed.

3

News Item: May 5, 1961 - Alan Shepard, in a Mercury spacecraft, achieved a 15-minute sub-orbital flight, becoming the first US astronaut in space.

News Item: February 20, 1962 - John Glenn, in the Mercury spacecraft Friendship 7, successfully completed three earth orbits, becoming the first US astronaut to orbit the earth.

News Item: May 15, 1963 - Gordon Cooper, in the spacecraft Faith 7, completed 22 orbits of the Earth in the last Mercury flight.

In the summer of 1963, two experimental engineers at IITRI in Chicago brainstormed the idea of building a rocket-powered supersonic land speed record vehicle. I was one of them.

Ray Dausman, working in Propellants Research, had just seen his first drag race that September and excitedly told me what he observed. He was impressed by the pulsating sounds of the fire-belching 1,200 horsepower engines, and clouds of white smoke billowing from the fat racing slicks, on dragsters sprinting down the black asphalt at the NHRA Summernationals. However, the resulting performance of the fuel dragsters seemed disappointing after all that chemical, mechanical, and human effort was expended. Speeds of 205 mph and elapsed times (ETs) of 7.5s were record-breaking 1/4 -mile performances at that time. But Ray suggested to me that a small rocket-powered car could do much better. This novel concept appealed to my competitive nature right away. We discussed the

4

rocket idea over the winter of 1963/'64, explored the technical literature, and then drove to FMC Corporation in Buffalo, New York to visit rocket engineer James McCormick and pick his brain in the early spring of 1964.

Some of the drag racing organizations had recently recognized a new 'unlimited' class for thrust-powered turbojet dragsters. Agreeing that a rocket-powered car was just about as unlimited as one could get, we decided to explore the potential of our idea. The Federation Internationale de l'Automobile or FIA (the international body governing auto racing) had also just opened the world's land speed record (LSR) to thrust-powered automobiles. In August 1963 Californian Craig Breedlove had driven his thrust-powered tricycle *Spirit of America* to 407.45 mph. Though the FIA refused to recognize that, the Federation Internationale Motocycliste or FIM (the international governing body of motorcycling) did, regarding Breedlove's remarkable projectile as a motorcycle and sidecar! Inevitably, the FIA had to accept the new breed of fast cars and its Category C belatedly recognized 'special' land vehicles - those that were thrust-powered and no longer driven through their wheels - for speed record attempts from 1964 onwards. This new ruling opened up the field for both turbojet and rocket motors.

It was Tom Green of Wheaton, Illinois who set the first official thrust-powered LSR on the Bonneville Salt Flats in Utah at 413.20 mph, with Walt Arfons' Goodyear-sponsored *Wingfoot Express* on October 2, 1964. Three days later Walt's estranged brother Art drove his Firestone-backed *Green Monster* to 434.02 mph before Breedlove came back to make his record official with 468.72 mph another eight days later, and then raised that to 526.28 mph two days on in a hair-raising ride when he lost his braking parachutes and ended up nose-diving into a brine lake.

Breedlove and Arfons fought a game of record roulette on the salt, with Arfons having the last word for 1964 at 536.71 mph a week after Breedlove's adventure. In November 1965 Craig regained his laurels at 555.483 mph in a new four-wheeled *Spirit of America – Sonic 1*, before Arfons replied with 576.553 mph five days later. Breedlove then beat Art to the next barrier with 600.601 mph on November 15. And there the record sat as Art's next challenge, late in 1966, ended in a horrendous accident in excess of 600 mph from which he was mighty lucky to survive unharmed.

It was Arfons' 536 mph record that first made us even more determined to look into an innovative rocket car concept. We saw opportunity knocking at our door if only we could move fast enough. A rocket would blow these jet cars away.

Lunch discussions between Ray and I in the IITRI cafeteria through the early months of 1964 had quickly became planning sessions with numerous sketches on napkins and busy work on our slide rules, while co-workers skeptically observed our growing obsession. Working together, doing the calculations, drawings and developing the Samarium Oxide coating process for the silver catalyst screens, we built a tiny hydrogen peroxide

H PR-25 25lb thrust test rocket

(H2O2) monopropellant rocket motor that developed 25 lbs of thrust.

Ray had been a student member of the American Rocket Society at Purdue University and collected several books on rocket design. Race car chassis engineering was one of my passions and my library included many dog-eared volumes on

6

Formula One, sports car, and Indianapolis car design. But we really had no money available to fund an ambitious project of this nature beyond building that little motor, so our enthusiasm was tempered a bit at the start by that reality. How can we do this, we wondered?

My father was the vice president of a major nationwide insurance company when I was growing up. Although he passed away while I was still in high school, he taught me some valuable lessons in life. Being a gear head by nature, I was not interested in becoming a businessman or salesman. A career in engineering beckoned. However, Dad convinced me that it was helpful to understand that 'salesmanship' was necessary regardless of one's career path. It was important to 'sell' yourself, to your employer, to your colleagues, and even to your own self, in order to attain important goals in life. Life's sales tools are knowledge, ambition, enthusiasm, and self-confidence. These give you credibility to convince others to help achieve what matters to you. Thankfully, I listened and learned.

So, it was easy to sell the already enthusiastic Ray on moving forward on the project. In September I had first mentioned the idea of a rocket car to Pete Farnsworth at a drag race, and we agreed to work on the project together after a meeting in October. Pete was a hot-rodder acquaintance of mine who drove and built dragsters professionally, and lived in Milwaukee, Wisconsin. That was where we met with him and were able to sell him on the idea to team with us building the rocket dragster. He had thought of building one himself for a few years, but when he saw our test films he was fascinated by our innovative hydrogen peroxide rocket design and agreed to join our venture. That was when we formulated a plan to attack the land speed record in a logical, scientific manner, proposing a three-phase program:

a) design and develop a scaleable small prototype rocket motor to demonstrate our competence as designers and builders of such a powerplant;

b) design and develop a prototype rocket-powered car with a scaled-up motor, as a design exercise, and to provide us and the driver with operating experience of a rocket-powered vehicle, and finally

c) design and construct the LSR vehicle itself, conduct preliminary testing, and then record attempts.

We first tested our rocket motor in the summer of 1964. It was only the size of a small vitamin pill bottle. We scrounged tubing and valves in the used equipment piles and found a surplus stainless-steel oxygen tank to hold the peroxide. I machined the stainless-steel rocket chamber and nozzle in the laboratory shop at night from bar stock 'donated' by IITRI. Using simple instrumentation consisting of my bathroom scale and 16 mm movie camera, we fired the motor several times. The first was behind the home of my friend Ray Muller in Blue Island, Illinois. Ray was part of the Speed Sports drag race group with Joe Bush and Don Maynard, building several dragsters. I was originally going to ask him to be our prototype rocket dragster builder before I later asked Pete to join us.

We refined the rocket until it performed to our specifications. Hearing that small motor roar the first time was breathtaking. No fire, no smoke, just the high-pitched note of the rocket's exhaust as I opened the fuel valve, and the rising thrust reading on the scale. We had done it! It was a small step, but the first important one in our journey. We were now rocket engineers.

HPR-25 rocket test stand

The prototype motor and test program cost us each several

hundred dollars. And although the results were more than convincing, we were two young men (25 years old, married, two children each) naturally reluctant to invest more of our limited family finances in such a risky venture.

But we were encouraged to continue our work by IITRI's Dr Wilson 'Bud' Whaley and Dr James Brophy, who was the Director of IITRI's Chemistry Research Division. I'd worked on Bud's G-Modified class Elva Climax sports racing car in local Chicago Region SCCA races for a few years and he knew my technical ability. Dad's sales lectures were beginning to show results.

With Dr Whaley's assistance, I prepared a modest project sponsorship proposal in January 1965 and Ray, Pete and I formed a partnership, DFK Enterprises. It wasn't incorporated, but we wanted some business identity to establish a bank account and for correspondence, etc. That month I began to present our proposal to several tire and chemical companies. Although some of the firms expressed polite interest, they wanted to see something more convincing than photographs of our tiny engine and theoretical performance calculations of a conceptual land speed record vehicle.

It was frustrating to see our brilliant idea dismissed out of hand by potential sponsors. They obviously didn't anticipate the benefit, which I tried to illustrate, of breaking the world's land speed record, breaking the sound barrier on land, and drawing the attention of the whole world's media to their partnership in a historic event. But even with the disappointing rejections, Ray and I became more convinced than ever we had to find a way to move our dream further to completion.

Our next step in the plan was to build a larger rocket engine and the prototype car. We'd design it to compete as an unlimited dragster, like the jet cars, and book it for exhibition races in the hope of earning enough money to pay us back. In January we began building the *X-1*.

I was working a series of part-time jobs, bartending, department store clerk, and pumping gas to help fund what had become an obsession. It was obvious to me that we were on the verge of creating a new paradigm for land speed racing. I had to see this through to the end. The speed bug had bitten me hard.

HPR-2500 2500lb thrust rocket assembly

Work on the prototype car began immediately. By the end of April we'd completed a 2500-lb thrust rocket motor (HPR-2500), scaling up our little prototype 100 times. Like the first motor, it was a catalytic monopropellant rocket using 90% (by weight) hydrogen peroxide (H_2O_2) decomposed over a silver-wire screen to produce thrust. Friends in IITRI's mechanical engineering prototype shop machined the parts in the evening after work hours. They were intrigued by our exciting project and volunteered their help. Ray and I fabricated the rocket catalyst pack in the chemical lab.

We incorporated Reaction Dynamics, Inc. in May to minimize our personal liability. Ray, Pete, and I were equal shareholders.

Since the rocket car was not wheel-driven, I designed it for light weight, low frontal area, and good handling. Weight transfer dominated conventional dragster design but wasn't a factor at all. It looked more like a Formula 1 or Indianapolis racer as a result. The car was of a contemporary spaced tube frame design for lightness and stiffness. It had four-wheel independent suspension and independent front and rear disk brake systems. Also, three ribbon braking parachutes provided retardation. Pete began building the chassis in his Milwaukee garage while Ray and I commuted from Chicago on weekends to help out and later install the rocket motor and plumbing. Before we were finished building the car, Ray had moved to Milwaukee to work at Allis-Chalmers on fuel cell research

X-1 frame on welding bench

News Item: March 23, 1965 - John Young and Virgil Grissom successfully orbited the Earth three times in their Gemini 3 spacecraft, the first US 2-man space flight.

X-1 assembled by Pete and Ray

Meanwhile, in autumn 1965, spurred on by the rapid escalation of speeds Breedlove and Arfons continued their duel in autumn 1965 at Bonneville, we finished building the *X-1* chassis in May, 1966. From this point forward we believed that time was of the essence if we were to be first to the sound barrier on land. We static-tested the rocket motor at Great Lakes Dragaway in the *X-1*, with me in the cockpit, rather than on a test stand. This saved considerable time and money without seriously compromising safety. Prior testing of the smaller prototype rocket assured me there would be no major safety hazard using this procedure. Even so, I hadn't slept a wink the night before.

The main purpose of these tests was to check flow rates, chamber pressure, and thrust. Sitting in the cockpit, I fastened the safety harness "just in case". Intently watching the pressure gauges, I slowly twisted the pressure regulator dome loader,

causing the gauge arrow to move clockwise, until I saw 600 psi in the peroxide tank. Now the rocket was armed and ready to shout. With the *X-1* chained down, I warmed up the catalyst by partially

X-1 chassis rear view

opening the throttle, and then opened it wide. The car rolled forward, lunging against the restraint and then held the chain taut

as the rocket barked. I was relieved when the fuel ran out a few seconds later and it was quiet once more, but I could hear my heart still racing. The thrust dynamometer telltale arrow showed we reached 2,500 lbs! Once again our design was

X-1 chassis front view

validated and we knew we were moving forward. Nothing would stop us now. Next, drive the car down the track.

I made two preliminary test runs in July, applying power for only a few seconds and then coasting to the end of the 1/4-

mile track before using the brakes, as we hadn't yet installed the parachutes. We filmed those two tests demonstrating my throttle control of the rocket. I staged the *X-1* at the starting line like a normal piston-engine dragster, and then checked the handling while allowing sufficient room to stop.

Pulling the hand throttle, I heard a hissing sound of propellant flowing into the rocket, then a low-pitched rumble as the car smoothly eased up to the line. So far, so good. The Christmas tree starting lights counted down to green – and I was off! With practically no sound in the cockpit I was squeezed back into my seat by an invisible hand until halfway down the track when the fuel ran out. Success! I was still alive. The car ran so smoothly there was practically no sensation of speed as I coasted to the turnoff lane at the end of the track. Charged with adrenalin, I was bathed in sweat when Pete threw me a nylon line for the tow back to the pits. While we refueled for the second run I was trembling with excitement. It all happened too quickly to recall any anomalies. On the second run I was more relaxed and able to steer the car a little from side to side after the power shut-off, checking for stability. It drove like it was on rails.

Having only driven my B/Gas sedan in drag races until then, it occurred to me that the *X-1* could easily be the fastest dragster in the world. It was more thrill than I was prepared to handle. I was overwhelmed by the thought of cruising down the strip at over 200 mph. If I could handle it, numerous expensive practice runs, building up speed, would be required before we could be competitive. This was not going to work.

After this we decided that an experienced professional driver should handle the X-1 for the high-speed tests that were to follow. We believed this driver could then be phased into the LSR program with minimal retraining. Chuck Suba of Calumet City, Illinois was a high school friend of mine and Pete's who had built and driven quite a variety of drag race vehicles, from motorcycles to turbojets. Chuck was immediately interested in the LSR project and agreed to drive the *X-1*, providing he would have the first option on driving the record attempt vehicle. We were now ready to go racing.

Chuck drove the car, still without its streamlined body, on September 5, 1966 to check out the high-speed characteristics of the chassis. The fuel load was limited to 100 lbs for all of the early runs. His best ride of the day resulted in a 7.19s elapsed time and a top speed of 203.39 mph. The test runs indicated minor suspension changes were necessary but all other systems operated perfectly. This was exciting because the fastest Top Fuel dragsters in the country at that time were not running quite that quick. Even so, our fuel supply was exhausted at about 900 ft, so that the car coasted through the last 400 of the 1/4-mile dragstrip. At the end of the day Chuck stood alongside the *X-1* shaking his head in amazement. This strange little machine performed beyond belief.

News Item: November 11, 1966 - James Lovell and Edwin Aldrin completed four days in earth orbit in their Gemini 12 spacecraft, last flight in the series.

News Item: January 27, 1967 - Fire during the countdown rehearsal of the first Apollo spacecraft claimed the lives of Virgil Grissom, Edward White, and Roger Chaffee.

The *X-1*'s body was completed in April, 1967. Pete had to form it himself after we found professional aluminum fabricators too expensive for Reaction Dynamics' modest budget. It was colored a patriotic red, white, and blue with red 'X-1' painted large on its side.

Chuck then made several 1/8-mile runs in order to verify the *X-1*'s aerodynamic stability with the enveloping body. I mounted a movie camera on the car to monitor suspension movement and parachute operation. As a result of these tests, we added air scoops at the rear to break up stagnant airflow behind the car which had made parachute deployment unreliable.

Pete and Ray Installing the X-1 hand-formed body shell

After these preliminary tests were finished we finally launched the completed *X-1*, once again with just 100 pounds of hydrogen peroxide propellant, at Rockford Dragway on August 13, 1967. In contrast to the roaring fuel dragsters and jets, the car sat quietly on the start line until the green light flashed on, then became a blur as it rocketed forward. It shot like a bullet down the track, shocking the audience who had never experienced

X-1 body assembled with Pete and

Pete and Ray adjusting X-1 on assembly bench

anything like this. Cameras clicked too late as the car was gone before the shutters could capture it. One run was made at 200 mph with an amazing ET of 6.30s, demolishing the track record of 7.10s, which had been set only the previous week. At

the time, the fastest accurately clocked 1/4-mile performance was set by Art Arfons' Green Monster at 258.62 mph and 6.79s. This was at the Bonneville Salt Flats where he could use over a mile to stop the car. However, the FIA

X-1 cockpit

18

X-1 with finished body and paint

had not begun to officially recognize 1/4-mile standing start speed records. Our X-1 (the first successful driver-controlled rocket-powered racing car) had thus demonstrated stunning potential on its first serious attempt at a dragstrip. We were elated as Chuck sprang from the cockpit with his toothy grin. It was beers all around

Ray, Chuck, Pete, and Dick with their X-1 completed

that night.

We encountered a minor problem during this run. The Plexiglas windshield shattered due to stresses at high speed halfway through it, cutting Chuck's nose. We then replaced it with a more flexible laminated Lexan material.

The following Sunday, August 20, the *X-1* made two runs at Route 30 Dragway in Crown Point, Indiana, just south of Chicago. Our new windshield failed again on the first attempt and Chuck released the parachutes before crossing the finish line. This resulted in a 6.57s ET (a new track record) with a very slow recorded speed of 160.714 mph. Chuck was anxious to run again even without the windshield. The facemask and goggles would protect his face from the wind adequately, so we decided to try it. Chuck gave Pete the thumbs-up sign as the car was pushed silently to the starting line again. The track timers announced an incredible ET of 5.41s for the *X-1*'s next run. This time was way quicker than what we had calculated

would be possible and was later thought to have been an error. While the actual ET was probably more like 6.4s, the lower figure was unfortunately publicized by the track promoter and

Chuck blasting off the starting line at U.S. 30 drag strip

national drag racing publications, causing major excitement in the racing community. This problem would continue, making it difficult for us developing the rocket car and meanwhile creating animosity in the jet car community.

X-1 dual parachutes deployed

Two weeks later, Chuck appeared with the *X-1* at an all-jet Labor Day weekend Drag Fest which lasted three days and took place at two nearby tracks, Great Lakes Dragaway in Wisconsin and Rockford Dragway in Illinois. Our little 750 lb *X-1* rocket car was to run 'round-robin', meeting each of the huge turbojet cars once during the series. The jet dragster owners, however, were not about to be made to look foolish by losing to our diminutive rocket car. They refused to race us. The *X-1's* reputation (and that erroneous 5.41s ET performance) had apparently spread across the country.

A compromise was reached. The jets would run each other in normal double-elimination style. The winner would have the 'honor' of racing Chuck and the *X-1* for 'Top Eliminator' title. The first race was on Saturday night. Pete and Ray had built a new, thicker, heat-formed Plexiglas windshield, which would be tested on the first warm-up run. Chuck whistled through the timing lights at 152 mph in 7.02s. The windshield remained intact. The *X-1* was ready to do battle.

Chuck was finally matched up against Doug Rose in Walt Arfons' *Green Monster* dragster (this was one of a series of cars of that name, but not to be confused with his brother's LSR car). Another last-minute compromise required the *Green Monster* to get a 1.5s handicap head start. The jet turned a 7.2s ET, beating the *X-1* in its first actual side-by-side competition although we turned a 6.78s ET and 229.29 mph.

The next day in Wisconsin featured more of the same. Chuck warmed up with a 6.42s (track record) run at 214.28 mph. He then raced Walt Arfons' *Exodus* Jet Eliminator winner. This time, the jet had only a 1s lead and it was close at the finish as Chuck roared through in 6.52s, losing again. The last race of the weekend series was again held at Rockford. Our fledgling Reaction Dynamics crew was fed up and determined to hold ground. If another unreasonable handicap were to be imposed, we would pack up and go home. Rose again won the Jet Eliminator category in the Green Monster. The crowd anxiously awaited the final showdown.

After much haggling, it was decided the *X-1* would allow Doug one-half second, so he could light his afterburner before Chuck rocketed down the track. When the Christmas tree went green in Doug's lane, the powerful fire-belching jet roared and lurched forward. Almost instantly, the powerful 'boom' of the afterburner could be felt the length of the track. Then the high-pitched scream of the rocket added to the bedlam of sound. The little *X-1* flashed past the roaring giant jet car about 500 ft from the start and pulled away. At about 1000 ft the rocket's roar stopped, as the restricted fuel supply was exhausted and the car began to slow down. The *Green Monster* began closing the gap, but Chuck shot past the finish line in 6.32s, the winner. Towing

X-1 being fueled at the drag strip

back on the return road past the grandstands, Chuck ceremoniously blew kisses to the spectators.

We now realized that our experiment was a success. Absolutely, we had built the fastest dragster in the world. Not only that, we were only showing a portion of the rocket's potential with the small fuel tank. Chuck had only dreamed of this moment since high school. He finally was truly at the pinnacle of his sport.

Our performances with the *X-1* would prove to be another very timely step in selling the LSR project. Unknown to me, Dr Bob Rosenberg, a director at my then-employer IGT, was watching intently in the grandstands. Bob had been listening to my rants at work about the *X-1* and our jet car battles. He was impressed at the ease with which we defeated the former world land speed record holder, Walt Arfons, and would become a great ally.

The *X-1* rocket made solo runs at a few Midwestern tracks after that, and wound up the season with a match race against Romeo Palamides' *Untouchable* jet dragster at Great Lakes Dragaway on October 22, 1967. The two-out-of-three race series was over in two runs as Chuck notched up yet another track record at 6.25s, although giving up 0.5s in handicaps both times.

Meanwhile, my rough calculations on the new LSR vehicle design concept indicated that the $H2O2$-fueled rocket motor was not energetic enough for achieving a supersonic record, which was what we had targeted from the very beginning. At that time I was working at the Institute of Gas Technology (IGT) at IIT and discussed using liquefied natural gas (LNG) as the fuel with $H2O2$ as an oxidizer. The natural gas industry was conducting studies of this new cryogenic clean-burning fuel at the IGT research laboratories, for use in aircraft and fleet vehicles. The performance potential of this proposed combination looked good, so with Dr Rosenberg's help I created a new sponsorship proposal to break the land speed record, using an LNG-fueled rocket motor, to put to the natural gas industry. We met with Northern Illinois Gas Company (NIGAS) executives in January, 1968 to look into our LSR project. NIGAS chairman Marvin Chandler agreed to pursue the LNG idea further within the industry. Our project was getting legs. This was fantastic. Now we had natural gas insiders selling the project for us to the industry through their national marketing organization, the American Gas Association (AGA). It was beginning to look a lot like we would do this thing. While we weren't making enough money racing the rocket dragster to build our LSR car, running it had opened the door to a real LSR sponsorship.

Chuck was feeling very comfortable now in the *X-1*, and insisted that we enlarge the propellant tank to 130 lbs capacity. The car had handled flawlessly so far, and he felt it was safe to try higher speeds. We always operated with the philosophy that stopping safely was more important than going fast. But we agreed this was a reasonable change now.

Our first run in 1968 was at Oswego Dragway in Illinois, on May 26. Oswego had a very short braking area past the timing lights, so we were somewhat apprehensive. However, we had all raced there many times and were familiar with the situation. It rained intermittently all day. Chuck sneaked in two solo runs between showers and the car's potential finally became apparent

Dual chutes stopping at Oswego drag strip

25

to us. The first cautious effort produced a 6.28s ET and 214.28 mph. The second time the sun peeked through the clouds, he was ready to go and powered through the timing lights at 257.14 mph in 6.03s. Rooster tails of water spumed off the tires as Chuck darted through puddles in the braking area, running off the end of the track into a Midwestern cornfield. He was laughing and pumping his fists in the air as we towed him through the cornstalks and down the road to the pits with bits of crops dangling

Off the end of the track at Oswego drag strip

Art Arfons' unofficial record of 6.79s ET and 258.62 mph was the next target for us. Rockford Dragway sponsored an attempt for us to break those marks on July 6. To assure accurate timing, Dick Paul of the Rockford strip had the dual Chrondek electronic timers re-calibrated at the factory. During the record attempts the clocks agreed to within 0.001s on each run. Since the track was sanctioned by the National Hot Rod Association (NHRA), drag racing's only FIA representation, this would be the first thrust-powered (though unofficial) record attempt under their auspices. The rules for this attempt would be that the average of two runs (in the same direction) would count toward the record. After a trackside interview with the commentator, Chuck climbed into the car and cranked out a 251.39 mph run in 6.21s. An hour later, the *X-1* was fuelled and sat on the starting line as the crowd counted down with the Christmas tree starting light. 6.072s later, it crossed the finish line at 248.61 mph. The average of 6.144s was touted as the 'official' record and Chuck had lowered the track record to 6.072s.

We were ecstatic now. These record times were finally accepted by a skeptical drag racing fraternity nationwide. We had bested another land speed record holder, Art Arfons. Our heroes were now our peers. Even so, we never were able to book the *X-1* outside the Midwestern states. The west coast racers considered us to either be hicks or phonies, or both. The east coast promoters were also quite parochial. We knew we would need a world land speed record to really prove our mettle.

After the Rockford race we decided to remove excess weight from the *X-1* to gain more acceleration and pursue still higher speeds. It wasn't until September that we would run the car again.

Meanwhile, the natural gas industry, through the AGA, began to consider our LSR program as a realistic possibility to promote LNG fuel and advanced us an initial small payment to kick start the project. In August, 1968 Reaction Dynamics began applying itself to meet the technical challenges involved in the LSR vehicle design. Consultants from the Mechanical and Aerospace Engineering faculty at IIT were hired to assist us with vital calculations in the propulsion system, structural design, and aerodynamics. We leased a small shop in Milwaukee as our headquarters where we would build our new car. With the help of some in-kind sponsorships, tools and fabricating equipment were acquired as the LSR project gained momentum. It was hard to believe, but we really were on our way.

Our last racing date of 1968 for the *X-1* was September 15 at Oklahoma City Dragway. We didn't realize then that this would be our grand finale. Another jet car championship was scheduled, and Chuck with our *X-1* was invited to race against Walt Arfons' new *Neptune* steam rocket, with the winner to race the Jet Eliminator winner. Several natural gas industry executives, potential sponsors, would be on hand to see Reaction Dynamics and the *X-1* in action.

Walt's steam rocket had a reputation of being dangerous to drive. I asked the promoter to have the driver, Duane Landon, make a solo pass to check it out before running against Chuck. The steam car roared away down the strip leaving a white vapor trail, veered out of control to the right, and rolled over at the end of the track. Exit one steam rocket! Wearing a blue dress shirt and tie to tweak the jet car drivers, Chuck climbed in the seat for his ride. The *X-1* then made a single run for Rocket Eliminator and the scoreboard lit up and showed 257.88 mph in 5.09s. Oh, no! Not again! That's all it took to freeze up the jet car owners. The whining began again.

Walt Arfons' *Green Monster*, now driven by Ted Austin, won the Jet Eliminator category. We again pushed Chuck and the *X-1* to the starting line, waiting for the *Green Monster* to show up for the speed duel. But Walt complained that it was embarrassing for his powerful fire-belching Unlimited Jet Dragster to run against the lightweight rocket car. The track promoter backed down and the little red, white, and blue racer was sent off on another solo run. This time Chuck really yanked hard on the throttle and soared through the photocell beams at 265.48 mph with an elapsed time of 4.90s. Now, our *X-1* was the quickest and the fastest dragster in the world. A later check of the timing equipment showed that the track operator had 'accidentally' left an electronic handicap timer plugged into the ET timer system, erroneously subtracting 1.000s from the actual times. 5.90s was still the best time ever recorded by far, and so was the speed. Once again we had routed the jet cars. Either way, we were elated. And so were the enthusiastic gas industry execs who had just given us their final approval to pursue the land speed record.

That was to be the end of the *X-1*'s drag racing career. It had been exciting and fun while it lasted. But now it was retired and we looked forward to racing in an environment where timing would be accurate and certified by an international authority, not phony records hyped by dragstrip promoters' 'happy clocks' of the era.

Our elation was to be tempered by sadness. One month later, on Sunday October 13, 1968, I settled down with my family in front of the TV to watch the Ed Sullivan Show. The telephone rang. When I answered, Pete spoke quietly. Chuck had been fatally injured at Rockford Dragway in a racing accident. While qualifying a piston-engine Top Fuel Dragster for an acquaintance, he lost control at high speed, slid off the track, and crashed into a finish line marker. On the same track where three months earlier he had triumphed, now he had

X-1 with Rislone sponsor decal

perished. I sat stunned for the rest of the evening. The sudden finality of his death was devastating.

We agreed not to discuss the situation further until after the funeral so that we could fully comprehend what had happened and how we should react. The funeral in Evanston, Illinois was somber, with a closed casket. All of the local racers and Chuck's friends filled the funeral parlor for two days. His parents and sister knew our bond with their son was strong since we had practically grown up together. They were consoling us as we were comforting them. We had hung out at the Suba's home as young adults and knew each other well. Chuck was like a brother to us in many ways, especially close since we were working together as team-mates. And now he was gone forever, but his memory lives on in our hearts even to this day. Why he decided to climb into that ill-handling dragster still mystifies us. But, that is what adventurous young men do – sometimes at their peril.

In addition to losing a close friend, we had lost our LSR driver. Even while we mourned Chuck, the gas industry began asking us what we intended to do. We needed to assure them we had a plan to complete the project. A search for a new driver commenced immediately. But the project would not be the same from then on.

By January, 1969 the entire Reaction Dynamics staff was at last working fulltime on our primary project, the rocket-powered car to set the World Land Speed Record. The American Gas Association, as well as most of the consumer natural gas companies, had some form of a blue gas flame as their logo. Even some gas appliances had a similar one. The AGA's PR firm believed that would give the sponsors immediate visual recognition, so now the big car had a name which incorporated that logo. We would call it *The Blue Flame.*

While intended as the prototype for a land speed record vehicle, our little *X-1* had ushered in a new era of drag racing – the Rocket Age – which would see unbelievable records set on drag strips across the US and in Europe in the years to come. Rocket dragsters would later also set numerous FIA World Records for standing start distances.

We really had created an exciting new paradigm in the space age.

-2-

THE BLUE FLAME WAS REALLY GREEN

Green? I thought it was blue?

Oh, I get it. Green, as in environmentally friendly.

The Blue Flame set the world land speed record at over 630 mph on October 23, 1970 using propellants that are still considered quite beneficial in these times of 'carbon footprint' sensitivity, liquefied natural gas (LNG) and hydrogen peroxide (H_2O_2).

Even back in 1970 it was recognized that clean-burning natural gas caused less atmospheric pollution than other contemporary fossil fuels. This is because it is essentially methane (CH_4), the simplest hydrocarbon molecule, having only one carbon atom.

There was a brief movement to consider use of natural gas in motor vehicles, primarily fleet vehicles, to improve urban air quality in America. Then, the auto industry developed better strategies to reduce controlled emissions with exhaust system catalysts, fuel injection, and onboard computer technology to keep gasoline and diesel fuel in the game. Research and pilot programs using natural gas in motor vehicles have continued until today there are some 120,000 to 150,000 natural gas-powered vehicles on the road in the US.

How was *The Blue Flame* rocket design developed?

In 1964 Ray Dausman and I were research technicians at IIT Research Institute (IITRI), a contract research division of Illinois Institute of Technology (IIT) in Chicago. IITRI was engaged in both industrial and government research in the fields of Chemistry, Physics, and Engineering. Ray worked in Propellants Chemistry research while I was working in Fine Particles research, a specialized area of Physical Chemistry. Ray's projects primarily involved developing new rocket propellants and measuring their characteristics under contract to NASA and the US Air Force. I was working on military satellite defense systems and NASA Saturn I and Saturn V rocket fuelling systems' integrity monitoring.

Although our laboratories were in different sections of the IITRI Chemistry Research building, we lived in the same on-campus faculty apartment building and ate lunch together on occasion in the IITRI cafeteria. I'd tell Ray about my interest in hotrodding and drag racing, relating how the fastest dragsters were producing unbelievable power using nitromethane fuel. Ray had never seen a drag race. However, that year while enjoying the Labor Day holiday at his parents' vacation home near Indianapolis, he ventured to the National Hot Rod Association (NHRA) Summer Nationals drag race championships. What he witnessed that day would change our lives forever.

The following week at lunch Ray related his experience at the drag race. "They made one heck of a noise, shooting flames from the exhaust, and smoked the tires. But, they really seemed to be quite inefficient."

I could scarcely believe what I was hearing. These were the fastest drag racing cars in the world! What could possibly be more impressive than that?

"So much of that chemical energy is just being wasted with the noise and heat and spinning tires. A rocket could harness that energy and use it much more effectively," Ray explained.

Well, how about that? So then I told Ray about the turbojet-powered cars that weren't allowed to compete at NHRA tracks, being raced by Walt and Art Arfons. These were the various *Green Monster* dragsters. The Arfons brothers had initially raced their *Monsters* with large aircraft piston engines. They apparently came to the same conclusion as Ray, however, that jet propulsion would be more efficient than wheel-driven dragsters. Their speeds were a little faster than the nitro-fuel-burning piston-engine cars, but they were big and heavy and the jet engines available on the military surplus market were low power and technologically obsolete. In fact, stopping these behemoths was more difficult than accelerating them. Huge braking parachutes were necessary to keep them safe.

"How can we use a rocket?" I asked Ray. "They can't be controlled, they always explode, and the exhaust fumes are toxic. Besides, they always seem to start very slow when we see them launching on TV."

So now we had defined the problems. Our intellectual curiosity was piqued, so next we started to research solutions. We had a unique resource at our disposal at IIT, the John Crerar Library, the largest engineering library in the country. Also, we had a supportive work environment that encouraged us to explore new solutions to engineering problems.

First, we needed to find propellants that were chemically stable (not explosive), not toxic so they could be handled in a public setting (the drag strip), and could be used in a rocket that would be throttle-controlled by the driver. Additionally, the rocket design should be scaleable so that small prototypes could be tested safely, and then enlarged to propel a full-sized race car. The propellant also needed to be sufficiently energetic, having a reasonably high specific impulse (Isp) that only a small tank volume (and weight) would be required.

Reviewing the technical literature, it was immediately clear that a liquid monopropellant was an ideal choice. Only one liquid would have to be controlled. Also, a monopropellant eliminated potential explosive issues with bipropellants should the fuel/oxidizer ratios be incorrect. A low operating temperature of the propellant system would simplify the design and construction of the rocket chamber and nozzle, especially if it didn't require cooling.

While there were a few possible choices, 90% concentration hydrogen peroxide (H_2O_2) was the immediate winner since its exhaust gases were water (H_2O) and oxygen (O_2), $[2\ H_2O_2 \rightarrow 2\ H_2O + O_2 + heat]$, and no foreseeable threat to the driver, crew, and spectators (nor the environment). Also, it could be decomposed using an inert catalyst of silver screens resulting in a specific impulse (Isp) of 132 seconds (pounds of thrust per pound of fuel per second). Because the maximum rocket chamber temperature at the exhaust throat would only be 1350°F, uncooled stainless steel could be used. The heat developed in the exothermic catalytic decomposition rapidly expands the developed gases in the rocket chamber, accelerating the gases through the nozzle, creating thrust for propulsion.

High strength hydrogen peroxide (HTP) was available at a reasonable cost from FMC Corporation in Buffalo, New York since it was being produced in propellant grade for the US military. It was sold in 300 lb net weight aluminum drums, a convenient size for transport with a race car. Ray and I then visited the FMC Inorganic Chemicals Division, talking with Jim McCormick, a chemical engineer who had experience using HTP in rocket applications for the military and NASA. He gave us some pointers on the system design and handling HTP in the field. With this background information in hand we drove back to Chicago to begin work on our rocket system.

We designed and built a 25-lb thrust prototype rocket in the IITRI chemistry laboratory workshop. HTP propellant was pushed into the rocket chamber through a ball valve under pressure from a gaseous nitrogen tank. Thrust was varied by opening and closing the valve which regulated the propellant flow. The HTP decomposed rapidly, flowing through the catalyst screens and expanded with an exothermic reaction, exiting through a DeLaval nozzle, producing thrust. The exhaust was clear and very loud.

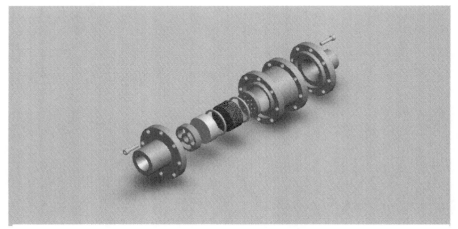

HPR-25 exploded view

HPR-25 section view

By now, we were excited and raised our sights a bit. A rocket dragster would be the next step, but a more ambitious final goal was developing, to challenge the world land speed record. In 1963 Craig Breedlove had set an unofficial new world record with his turbojet-powered *Spirit of America*, the first successful thrust-powered land speed record (LSR) vehicle. In 1964, Art Arfons and Tom Green challenged Breedlove in a duel at the Bonneville Salt Flats, Art finally finishing the year with his *Green Monster* holding the record after all three had been successful to varying degrees. Thrust cars were finally recognized by the international auto racing authorities that year and we rocketeers saw this as an opening for an even better solution to reaching the ultimate goal, exceeding the speed of sound on land.

Ray comparing HPR-25 to HPR-2500 in the X-1

The 25-lb thrust rocket design was scaled up 100 times, to 2,500 lbs thrust, and parts were fabricated in the IITRI Engineering Research machine shop. Joining forces with Pete Farnsworth, a drag racer and chassis builder, Pete, Ray and I formed Reaction Dynamics, Inc. and the *X-1* prototype rocket dragster was designed and built in Milwaukee. Our friend Chuck Suba drove it on drag strips, setting track records every time he raced.

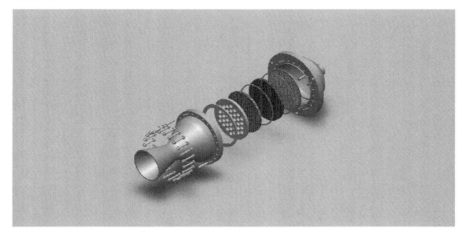

HPR-2500 exploded view

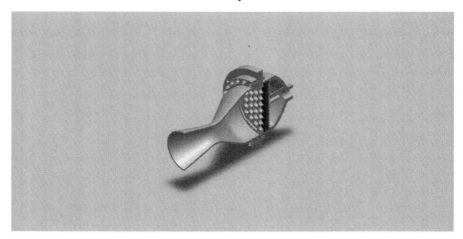

HPR-2500 section view

While a monopropellant HTP rocket had real potential for the land speed record design, a more energetic propellant would allow a smaller and lighter vehicle design. Since hydrogen peroxide decomposition resulted in a large volume of free oxygen being formed, a suitable hydrocarbon fuel could be burned in the rocket combustion chamber, increasing the thrust.

I was now working in combustion research at the Institute of Gas Technology (IGT), a contract research facility for the natural gas industry and also a part of IIT. The industry was then working on various ways to increase the awareness and use of natural gas in transportation, both on land and in the air. Liquefied natural gas (LNG) was an interesting alternative fuel being considered for its cryogenic cooling characteristics as well as its clean burning.

Several of the managers at IGT were aware of our *X-1* rocket dragster's successes and so I suggested to them a dynamic way to publicize LNG – a supersonic land speed record. Key gas industry executives were approached with a proposal to use LNG fuel, and they agreed to back the project, and thus began *The Blue Flame* record attempt.

One of the compelling reasons to use rocket propulsion for a land speed record vehicle was, rather than relying on finding a suitable surplus turbojet, we could design to whatever power output would be required for the task at hand. Another important consideration was aerodynamics. Rockets carry their own oxygen and don't require an air inlet which can increase drag and, also, can be quite difficult to design for transonic and supersonic speeds.

Setting a goal of 22,000 lbs thrust ultimately to produce an 850 mph design speed, a novel bipropellant rocket design began. Now some of the difficulties that had driven our original selection of a simple monopropellant rocket design would have to be addressed. The liquid bipropellant rocket system would have to control both an oxidizer (H2O2) and a fuel (LNG) in correct ratios. Also, the increased combustion temperature would require a cooling system to avoid melting the combustion chamber.

The Blue Flame's rocket design was unique and requires some explanation. It was designed with three possible operating modes. First, it could be run as a monopropellant HTP rocket producing 12,400 lbs of thrust. Then there were two additional modes, the first with LNG pre-heated to a gas phase in a heat exchanger downstream from the HTP catalytic decomposition before being injected into the hot oxygen-rich gas stream. This increased the chamber temperature and boosted the power to 16,000 lbs of thrust with an Isp of 171. Finally, a set of LNG

Ray working on HP-LNG-22000-V design

injectors downstream from the heat exchanger would add even more LNG, in liquid phase (analogous to the afterburner in a turbojet), to provide maximum thrust of 22,000 lbs of thrust and an Isp near 240.

Because Goodyear Tire and Rubber Company provided special racing tires for the record attempts with the condition that a speed of 700 mph should not be exceeded initially, it was decided not to use the liquid phase injectors, thus limiting the maximum speed. To reduce the car's weight under that restriction the LNG tank was downsized from 75 gallons capacity to just 10 gallons for 1970.

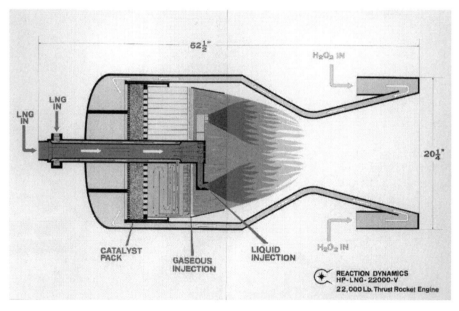

HP-LNG-22000-V bi-propellant rocket cutaway view

HP-LNG-22000-V front view

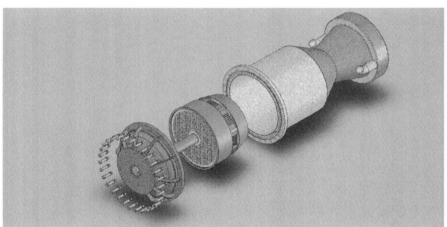

HP-LNG-22000-V exploded view

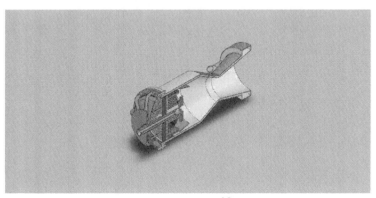

*HP-
LNG-
22000-V
section*

HP-LNG-22000-V hydrogen peroxide cooling jacket

LNG liquid injectors

44

Ray looking at the LNG heat exchanger array

Ray's height is compared to the HP-LNG-22000-V rocket. Large hoses route the hydrogen peroxide to the cooling jacket inlet.

WHY LNG?

What is Natural Gas?

Natural gas is a fossil fuel, meaning that it is derived from organic material deposited and buried in the earth millions of years ago. Natural gas comes from resulting reservoirs beneath the earth's surface. Sometimes it occurs naturally and is produced by itself (non-associated gas), sometimes it comes to the surface with crude oil (associated gas), and sometimes it is produced continually such as in landfill gas. Other fossil fuels are coal and crude oil. Together crude oil and gas constitute a type of fossil fuel known as 'hydrocarbons' because the molecules in these fuels are combinations of hydrogen (H) and carbon (C) atoms.

Renewable natural gas can also be produced from any organic waste or energy crop such as switchgrass. It's been conservatively estimated that America could produce 1.2 quadrillion Btus of renewable natural gas (also called biomethane). That's the equivalent of 10 billion gallons of gasoline. And, if making biomethane from cellulosic energy crops is considered, the potential is almost limitless.

The main component of natural gas is methane. Methane is composed of one carbon and four hydrogen atoms (CH4). When natural gas is produced from the earth, it is mixed with many other hydrocarbon molecules, like ethane (used for manufacturing), propane (which we commonly use for barbecues) and butane (used in lighters), which can be extracted for separate markets. Impurities containing small quantities of nitrogen, oxygen, carbon dioxide, sulfur compounds, and water may also be found in natural gas.

Natural gas supplies nearly one-quarter of US energy, according to the American Gas Association. The nation consumed 22.4 trillion cu ft in 2004; experts say consumption will increase by 20 per cent by 2030. Most natural gas demand comes from electricity generators because it is considered the cleanest-burning fossil fuel.

According to the Natural Gas Vehicles for America (NGVA), there are more than 120,000 natural gas vehicles on US roads. Fifty different manufacturers produce 150 models of light, medium and heavy-duty vehicles and engines, with about 22 per cent of all new transit bus orders requesting natural gas. Ninety-seven per cent of the natural gas used in America is produced in North America (85 per cent from the United States and 12 per cent from Canada).

We find natural gas around the world by exploring for it in the earth's crust and then drilling wells to produce it. Natural gas can be transported over long distances in pipelines or, as LNG, transported in ships across oceans. Natural gas can be stored until needed in underground caverns and reservoirs or as LNG in atmospheric tanks.

What is LNG?

Liquefied natural gas (LNG) is natural gas that has been cooled to the point that it condenses to a cryogenic liquid, which occurs at a temperature of approximately -256°F (-161°C) and at atmospheric pressure. The term 'cryogenic' means it boils at a low temperature, generally below -100°F. LNG is a clear liquid, with a density of about 45 per cent the density of water. Liquefaction reduces the gas volume by approximately 600 times, or 1/600th of the space required for a comparable amount of gas at room temperature and atmospheric pressure. This makes it more economical to transport between continents in specially designed ocean vessels. LNG technology makes natural gas available throughout the world.

To make LNG available for use, energy companies must invest in a number of different operations that are highly linked and dependent upon one another. The major stages of the LNG value chain, excluding pipeline operations between the stages, comprise the following:

- Exploration - to find natural gas in the earth's crust and production of the gas for delivery to users. Most of the time natural gas is discovered during the search for oil.

- Liquefaction - to convert natural gas into a liquid state so that it can be transported in ships.

- Shipping - to contain LNG in special-purpose vessels.

- Storage and Re-gasification - to convert the LNG stored in specially made storage tanks, from the liquefied phase to the gaseous phase, ready to be moved to the final destination through the natural gas pipeline system.

LNG Liquefaction

Feed gas to the liquefaction plant comes from the production field. The contaminants found in produced natural gas are removed to avoid freezing and damaging equipment when the gas is cooled to LNG temperature (-256°F) and to meet pipeline specifications at the delivery point. The liquefaction process can be designed to purify the LNG to almost 100 per cent methane. The liquefaction process entails cooling the clean feed gas by using refrigerants. The liquefaction plant may consist of several parallel units ('trains'). The natural gas is thereby liquefied for shipping at a temperature of approximately -256°F.

The LNG is stored in double-walled tanks at atmospheric pressure. The storage tank is really a tank within a tank that is filled with insulation, sort of a large Thermos bottle. The inner tank, in contact with the LNG, is made of materials suitable for cryogenic service and structural loading of LNG. These materials include 9 per cent nickel steel, aluminum and pre-stressed concrete. The outer tank is generally made of carbon steel or pre-stressed concrete.

What is Hydrogen Peroxide Propellant Grade?

Hydrogen peroxide (H2O2) was discovered by Louis-Jacques Thenard in July, 1818 and was described as 'oxygenated water'. While other chemists had produced H2O2 at approximately the same time as Thenard, he was the first to identify it and to define a procedure to manufacture it.

Rocket Propellant

The first major exploitation of hydrogen peroxide as a working fluid for propellant application is attributed to Hellmuth Walter. Walter created a company in 1935 to use 80% H2O2 as a propellant (at that time the highest concentration ever made in practical quantities). He started with submarine turbine drive systems and assisted take-off units (ATOs, also known as JATOs or RATOs) for military aircraft.

During the first large scale US propellant utilization of H2O2 (sometimes called HTP) in the Forties to Sixties three manufacturing processes predominated: electrolytic, anthroquinone, and oxidation of propane or propane derivatives. These processes were used in sufficient industrial capacity to produce large quantities of the chemical for both commercial and propellant grade uses. Each process was nominally associated with a particular supplier.

The electrolytic process for propellant grade H2O2 was primarily used by Becco/FMC in Buffalo, New York because of the nearby inexpensive source of hydroelectric power.

Electrolytic Process

The electrolytic process is an inorganic electro-chemical reaction, which involves the use of peroxydisulfuric compounds. One example is the method for which the basic reaction is:

1) $H_2S_2O_8 + H_2O \rightarrow H_2SO_5 + H_2SO_4$

2) $H_2SO_5 + H_2O \rightarrow H_2SO_4 + H_2O_2$

Reaction Control Systems

A heavily utilized area of H_2O_2 propulsion was as a Reaction Control System (RCS) monopropellant thruster. H_2O_2 was basically the first common aerospace monopropellant and was used on many of the early spacecraft and high altitude X-vehicles. It later would be replaced by hydrazine when the technical issues for that monopropellant were resolved. Some of the more notable RCS systems were the *X-1* and the *X-15* rocket-powered research aircraft.

The *X-1* RCS used 90% H_2O_2 thrusters made by Bell Aircraft Co. The thrusters operated across the range of 5 to 75 lb thrust (lb thrust) with specific impulses of 104 (@20 lb thrust,) and 118 (@42 lb thrust).

The *X-15* used H_2O_2 for attitude control with 4 pairs of 90% H_2O_2 mono-propellant rocket engines (a total of eight engines).

Later, monopropellant thrusters using hydrazine (N_2H_4) were commonly used on a variety of spacecraft and satellites. However, hydrazine is a highly toxic and dangerously unstable substance. Importantly, its use as a propellant has been compromised by stringent laws to protect personnel who have to work with substances which are highly toxic and carcinogenic.

Much more benign, low toxicity ('green') storable liquid propellants, such as H_2O_2, have therefore attracted considerable attention as possible replacements for hydrazine. This is due to the significant increase in the costs of production, storage and handling of these more toxic propellants, and has set the stage for green replacement propellants.

H_2O_2 continues to be one of the most attractive replacements, not only since it is non-toxic and non-carcinogenic, but also due to its many advantageous properties, such as its high density and relatively low cost. From a financial standpoint, H_2O_2 also promises significant cost savings due to the drastic simplifications in health and safety protection procedures during the production, storage and handling of the propellant.

-3-

CHUCK SUBA - THE ORIGINAL ROCKETMAN

During the Fifties and Sixties drag racing was still very much a grassroots sport. Do-it-yourself was the normal modus operandi. Racers Howard Carpenter and Jake Schuljak recalled: "To get enough money and combined skills to build a competitive race car, nearly all of the teams were partnerships. There were Cook & Bedwell, Cyr & Hopper, and Stone, Woods, and Cook to name a few nationally known cars."

"In Chicagoland, Chuck Suba's Evanston shop in the alley behind his parents' home at 922 Sherman Avenue was a gathering place for many drag race pioneers at that time", recalled Howard. These included racers such as Don Garlits, Art Malone, Pete Farnsworth, and hotrodder entrepreneurs such as Bob Stange (Strange Engineering) and Ed Stoffels (Quartermaster Chassis), who worked on their cars, exchanged technical information, and bench-raced into the late evenings. Suba was the 'Pied Piper' of Midwestern drag racing, hosting an informal forum of speed and horsepower.

Chuck (Sr.) and Jean Suba had been thrilled to have a healthy baby boy, Charles Manford Suba, crying in their arms in Evanston's St Francis Hospital on April 23, 1938. The Great Depression was winding down and the threat of war hadn't appeared yet. Baby Suba would be called 'Tommy' in his early years to avoid confusion with his father, but 'Chuck' would emerge in junior high school.

The Suba family encouraged little Tommy as he began to develop a curiosity, and then a passion, for making things go fast and then faster. He began with small jet-powered boats (which used baking soda pellets) in the bathtub, building model airplanes, CO_2-powered model race cars, and a motorized bicycle. While Tommy played baseball, basketball, and other sports with his grammar school classmates, it was piston engines and speed that captured his imagination.

In 1947 his little sister, Jean Ann, was born. The Suba's seemed to lack imagination in naming their offspring. While playing with her tea sets and wearing her mother's high heels and dresses she was continually annoyed by all the mess and noise Tommy created with his mechanical preoccupation. Her big brother had a quiet, fraternal affection for his pesky sibling. Near Christmas, while they were on a 'looking trip' to her favorite toy store in Evanston, she spotted a very special doll. Santa had already spent his modest budget on the Suba children at Sears. Chuck took note as they went home empty-handed.

Chuck Suba's hot rod Ford with Chuck Sr. and sister Jean Anne

Jean Ann recalls: "That doll just showed up on Christmas morning." Santa was surprised, too, as Tommy smiled quietly and watched joyful tears rolling down her cheeks.

Finally Chuck began to develop his knowledge and skills working on the real deal. Like most young hotrodders at that time he joined a car club while in high school, the Drag Links, to socialize and learn more about his hobby. Saving money from caddying and odd jobs, he built a flashy customized 1949 Ford coupe which was painted a brilliant red. Dad upholstered this first manifestation of his automotive creativity - as he would many of his son's subsequent creations.

Graduating from Evanston Township High School in 1956, Chuck moved on to study at Illinois College in Jacksonville. This is a small rural liberal arts college with distinguished alumni that includes William Jennings Bryan who, at the turn of the century, ran three times as the Democratic candidate for President of the United States. Chuck had sold his lovely coupe to help pay tuition and buy a used 1953 Triumph motorcycle for transportation. His room-mates continually complained about the

Chuck Suba Evanston High School 1956 yearbook graduation photo

greasy motorcycle parts scattered around the dorm as he tried to coax more power out of the ancient twin after class.

Looking for a way to finance his college tuition and study mechanical engineering, in 1956 Chuck applied to the GM Institute in Flint, Michigan to join their co-op engineering program. He left Illinois College when he thought he was accepted at GMI, but the co-op sponsor ultimately declined, so it was time to go to work. Soon after, his father was diagnosed with diabetes and Chuck told Jean Ann, "Now with the Old Man sick I just might have to get a real job." Moving back home, he worked at the Humphrey Chevrolet dealer's service department and was rapidly promoted to the service manager position. That was not destined to last long.

Chuck's first drag racer

By now Chuck had saved enough capital to really make some speed. Chuck's Precision Engines was born in the alley behind his father's Veterans Upholstery business at 1419 Sherman in Evanston. He also souped up his old Triumph to make real horsepower and show his technical prowess at the drag strip. On April 20, 1958 the five year-old 40 cu in Triumph set the elapsed time record at Great Lakes Dragaway in 10.38s at over 121 mph. The nitromethane-fueled bike was always in the top eliminator finals that summer, often winning. In those days all classes of vehicles could run off for the overall winner and the motorcycle's superior power to weight ratio made it very competitive.

With uncanny foresight, the May 23, 1958 issue of Drag Times, containing Chuck's Precision Engines' advertisement selling his Triumph drag bike, also ran this cartoon.

**DRAG TIMES
MAY 23, 1958**

When the dragstrip wasn't available, there were impromptu races on Evanston's north side streets to pass the time. McCormick Boulevard between Oakton and Howard (separating Evanston and Skokie) was a favorite venue and, for a while, the Edens Expressway also saw some illicit speed events. After leaving the Pie Pan Restaurant at Peterson and Cicero, racing from the Edens Expressway's Devon Avenue overpass northward to Touhy was a relatively safe route. A few times in 1957 while the Edens was temporarily shut down for repairs, Chuck and his buddy Bob Stange held drag races on their motorcycles. Once, after going neck and neck at 100 mph, Stange backed off only to see Chuck keep on the gas and reaching 120 to 130. Chuck had caught his front wheel in a pavement crack and kept accelerating, claiming "I was afraid I'd fall if I backed off."

While the shop behind Chuck Sr.'s business, Veterans Upholstery, was Chuck's commercial business address, the real action was taking place in the multi-car garage behind his parent's house, farther south on Sherman. There, Chuck assembled a complete machine shop for modifying engines and building cars.

I had first met him briefly in 1955 while I was attending St George High School, also on Sherman Avenue, and right behind St Francis Hospital. In those days we always wore our hotrod club jackets and he noticed my Igniters Auto Club colors while in the neighborhood after school.

"Who are the Igniters?" came a voice from behind as I was walking toward the Howard Street and Western CTA bus terminal after school. Turning around, I saw a crew-cut guy with a toothy smile wearing horn-rimmed glasses and driving a real cool 1949 Ford customized coupe. He offered me a lift for the few blocks. We talked about cars and drag racing, but I lived in Chicago, not Evanston, so we were never really acquaintances then. That was eventually to change.

Don Garlits of Tampa, Florida was the fastest Top Fuel Dragster racer of the day in 1958 and a friend of mine. We had arranged that I would help him work on his Swamp Rat at the ATAA World Series of Drag racing at Cordova, Illinois late in August and the following week at the AHRA National Championship in Great Bend, Kansas. These were two of several major drag races at that time which allowed fuel (nitromethane and alcohol) classes to run, while the NHRA had banned fuel as too dangerous and only permitted gasoline classes at their tracks.

Chuck Suba and his racing partner, Nicky Bogdan, were at Cordova watching the fuel dragsters and gathering ideas for a new car they were building in Chuck's shop. Although Garlits recorded top speed for the race, an exploding clutch in the last round of eliminations denied him the overall win. Suba immediately offered the use of his shop for us to repair the *Swamp Rat* and get ready for our trip to Kansas. While there, Don freely offered tuning tips to Chuck on how to run 98% nitromethane in his Chrysler dragster. At the end of the week Don, his wife Pat, and I headed out to Great Bend while Chuck and Nicky worked on revising their carburetors and getting the dragster ready to race.

Chuck's first dragster frame, partnered with Nicky Bogden

Tragically, later that fall Nicky was killed when their dragster crashed at Great Lakes Dragaway. The cause has remained a mystery as the race car just seemed to drive off the side of the track at the finish line. He had just completed an easy run clocked at 141 mph when the vehicle veered left, plowing nearly a quarter of a mile through an adjoining field. He suffered a fractured skull and broken neck. The Chrysler hemi engine

Chrysler v-8 in Chuck's dragster

was torn from the machine as it bounced against a pile of rocks in the farmer's field. The car was totally demolished.

For the next few years Chuck's shop became a racers' hangout in the evenings while he tuned engines in the daytime. Chowing down on bags of White Castle sliders and Cokes, we local hotrodders would tell funny stories and brag about how fast our cars would go. On Friday nights we would crowd into Chuck's bedroom with our pints of Peacock ice cream to watch 'creature features' on TV while his parents were shaking their heads in amusement in the living room. In those days 'nerds' played with mechanical things since video games and personal computers hadn't been invented.

Garlits was a frequent visitor to Chuck's Precision Engines, "I first got to know Chuck after that 1958 race in Cordova when we went to his shop in Evanston," he recalled. "The following year I was in Chicago and then went over to his place. I parked the race car trailer in his alley and worked on *Swamp Rat I*. While Suba and I worked on the car, he noticed it needed a little weld on the frame rail. Chuck said, "I know a guy right down the alley here that is a real good welder." He came out and welded it up for me. It was Bob Stange, who is now the biggest supplier of racing drive train components at Strange Engineering.

"Suba came down to Florida for a while in 1960. I was visiting him in Chicago and he had one of those Lincolns like the one that won the 1954 Pan American road race, the Carrera Panamericana, and said 'Let's go to Florida.' We got in that Lincoln and it handled real good on those old narrow country roads, pre-interstate highway days. In the middle of the night in Georgia - at 100 mph - we saw a smudge pot's dim orange flame on the road shoulder illuminating a little sign 'BRIDGE OUT, 500 FEET'. No way could we stop so I drove down into a ravine. We got a wrecker to pull us out. We'd hurt the front end, so we put it together good enough at a local junk yard where we could drive on to Florida. I'm still driving, and I pull into the new 12200 Nebraska Avenue speed shop's back driveway, which dead ended at the balancing shop. I stepped on to the brake and it went right to the floor. The brake line had been partially severed in the accident and we didn't catch it, and that was where it finally gave up. The Lincoln drove right into the building – took the whole front concrete wall out. That was the end of the Lincoln. We could have both been killed in Georgia! Chuck was fit to be tied. He didn't have anything to do, so he got a bunch of polishing equipment then came into the shop and showed us how to polish the magnesium wheels and stuff so they looked pretty. Then he hopped on a Greyhound back to Chicago.

"When we raced in the Chicago area, Oswego and so on, Chuck would always come out and help us. He was a great guy. I loved him!"

Ed Stoffels remembers: "I first met Chuck at the Union Grove dragstrip around 1956. I worked as a machinist at Erickson's Speed Shop on Irving Park Road and Chuck would come over often to visit.

"I bought that factory-modified 1954 Lincoln Capri in 1958 from a good friend of Ray Erickson's. He was a somewhat eccentric car nut who took a liking to me and gave me a great deal on it when he tired of it. It had a GM Hydramatic transmission, beefed up suspension, and modified carbs, cam and ignition. Chuck drove the car while I was in Marine Corps boot camp. I wish I had it today."

Chuck then partnered with Gene Burcham and their union was renamed Chuck & Gene's Precision Engines. They worked primarily on building and tuning engines for drag racers, for both street races and the dragstrip. They also built a Chrysler-powered dragster to promote their shop and get some thrills, but had very little time to run it.

Stoffels continued: "Dragsters powered by military surplus turbojets were being pioneered at that time by the brothers Arfons (*Green Monsters*), Romeo Palamides (*Untouchable*), and Bill Fredricks (*Valkyrie*). I enlisted in the Marine Corps in October of 1960 with another friend of mine. I wanted to get my service obligation done, but on my terms. I was promised that I would be trained as a jet mechanic (MOS 6412) and the Corps kept their promise. When I told Chuck about the jet mechanics schooling he became interested and decided to enlist, too. I think the Army was chasing him (Universal Military Training and Service Act was the law of the land at the time). Chuck didn't enjoy the structured life of the Marine Corps and I think he was later able to get an early discharge."

Following his active duty Chuck serviced the military jet aircraft at nearby Glenview Naval Air Station for a few years, as a part-time reservist, and continued his dragster building and tuning at Chuck & Gene's Precision Engines in Evanston.

Ed Stoffels introduced Chuck to Jake Schuljak in 1962, who asked him to tune his gas class Chevy-powered modified coupe drag racer. When approached by Jake, Chuck laughed and said "Gasoline is for cleaning parts." So, eventually out went the

Chevy and in went a proper Chrysler hemi running on nitromethane, and a productive partnership ensued. Over the next two years the Schuljak-Suba Bantam-bodied Fuel Modified Coupe held the Drag News 'Standard 1320' records in two classes with speeds over 180 mph.

Schuljak-Suba champion Fuel Coupe dragster

During this time I was working at IIT Research Institute in the chemistry research department. We had heard rumors that Chris 'The Greek' Karamesines was turning very fast times running the rocket propellant hydrazine in his dragster. Chuck asked me about it. But I suggested trying unsymmetrical dimethyl hydrazine (UDMH), also a rocket propellant that was less toxic and more stable. After I gave him a couple gallons of UDMH I never heard further about it.

Meanwhile, while racing out on the west coast, Chuck built two new Chrysler race engines for the coupe in (camshaft manufacturer) Ed Iskenderian's shop. Chuck told Jake, "This thing's really gonna go. If it holds together, hang on to your teeth!" That weekend they took the car to the San Gabriel dragstrip to race.

"It left like a banshee", Jake recalls. "People kept saying they never saw a car smoke the tires so hard." Unfortunately, it didn't hold together, spitting out a couple of connecting rods halfway down the strip. "Chuck was amazing with tuning race cars. Everybody in northwest Indiana bowed to him. Whatever he said to do, it worked."

Like most 'professional' drag racers in those days, the lads kept their day jobs. Theisen's Bar-B-Q restaurant in Calumet City sponsored the coupe and provided shop space. Part of the arrangement was to keep Tom Theisen's son occupied and out of the trouble that idle teenagers might find. In those days Calumet City was a wide open mob-controlled Chicago suburb with gambling, strip clubs, and prostitution rampant. Jake managed to find them carpenter jobs, subcontracting to install metal shingle roofing on commercial buildings.

Jake remembers: "Theisen bought a Rod Stuckey dragster chassis for us in the summer of 1963. We put one of those

Schuljak-Suba "Messerschmitt" Fuel Coupe dragster

64

Yes, there was a Messerschmitt body on the dragster

spare Bantam motors in the car, and then installed a Messerschmitt coupe body on it.

Messerschmitts were those weird little Fifties-era European bubble cars, and very narrow, as it was a tandem passenger design. We went to Bakersfield, California for the US Fuel & Gas Championship in early March of 1964. I drove the car to the AA Fuel Modified Coupe class win with a 9.01s ET and 179.81 mph speed. We also were voted the outstanding Fuel Coupe."

The jets, however, were beckoning Chuck and at last he succumbed. On the trip home from Bakersfield he drove down to Tucson, Arizona to look through the giant military surplus aircraft depot next to the Davis-Montham Air Force Base for suitable jet engines. Spying a J46 powerplant in good condition, he hauled it

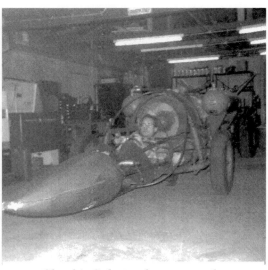

Chuck's Subajet dragster under construction

65

over to the nearby Tucson Speed Sport shop and, together with Red Greth and Lyle Fisher, began building a new jet dragster,

Jake continues: "After we all came back from Bakersfield with the Messerschmitt we had a full nose built and painted it

Head on view of the Subajet

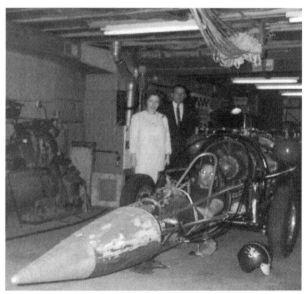

Chuck's SubaJet dragster with Mom and Dad looking on proudly

candy apple cherry red, a really sharp looking car for those days. The last run I made in it was at Cordova, at 185 mph. I lost the braking parachute, and crashed off the end of the track. Chuck, remembering Nicky's horrible accident six years earlier, wouldn't come down to see if I was okay. Finally, the safety crew gave him the okay sign and he brought the trailer down to load up the wrecked coupe. It was sold for parts."

Subajet on the trailer, ready to go racing

In an interesting twist of fate, the *Valkyrie* jet dragster that had been driven by a teenage Gary Gabelich was sold to Mickey Thompson, renamed the *US-1*, and then sold again to Art Malone. Mickey wanted to sell the car because it kept getting sideways at the end of the quarter mile. Chuck had heard this and encouraged Art to buy the car which they picked up and towed to the Oakland airport near San Francisco. There they checked out the jet engine and then towed it to Art's shop in

Indianapolis where they modified the rollcage and tried to improve the handling. Art was driving USAC Indy cars at the time and had a base there. After a few repairs and the modifications, they static tested the *US-1* at the Indianapolis drag strip. Roger 'Lucky' Harris was a good friend of Art's and wanted to drive

Subajet finished front view on the trailer

the car. "On a test run, Harris opened it up and it spun out in the lights," recalled Art.

Overcoming Malone's argument to forget the car until it could be straightened out; soon afterward Lucky drove it to a

Subajet on the road

win in a four-car-wide jet car drag race at Fontana, but spun it out again while slowing down. "That's it", Art hollered, "Park it until it's right – or forever!" Lucky insisted he would drive the car at a booked date in Islip, New York first. Malone told Lucky, "You're paid to drive this thing 1/8th mile. Don't try to impress some sweet thing in the stands by going the full quarter." Not listening to his

68

orders, Lucky spun out once again, crashed into the guardrail, and was killed instantly.

After Lucky Harris ran out of luck on June 3, 1966, the *US-1* was for sale again. Jake and Howard Carpenter, convinced this was a good thing by the persuasive Suba, mortgaged their homes to raise the $6,300 he needed to purchase the second jet dragster. Jake and Chuck could then match race the jet pair on the exhibition circuit.

Before the *US-1* would be run again, several changes had to be made to increase driver safety and engine reliability. Another attraction would soon change Chuck's direction in pursuit of the speed demon.

Jake recalled: "We picked up the *US-1* while Chuck was still finishing his *Super Jet* with the idea we would match race them together as an exhibition event at drag strips across the country. But before that happened, the rocket came along and the *Super Jet* then took a back seat."

Chuck's US-1 jet dragster unloading from the trailer

Business end of the US-1 jet dragster

Pete Farnsworth, Ray Dausman, and I were completing our *X-1* rocket powered dragster in Milwaukee and created Reaction Dynamics, Inc. The *X-1* was a prototype vehicle demonstrating a throttleable rocket powerplant designed to break the world's land speed record. Using monopropellant hydrogen peroxide fuel which decomposed to exhaust oxygen and water at a high velocity, and produced tremendous thrust, the *X-1* had first been tested in July of 1966. I drove the car, sans parachutes, with a half load of fuel on two test runs at Great Lakes Dragaway, demonstrating the power and controllability. Now, our trio of innovators was looking for a capable driver to show off the performance potential of this new concept.

Since I knew Chuck well and was still living in Chicago, I traveled south to Calumet City and made him an offer: "Drive the *X-1* on the drag strips to help us find the land speed record sponsorship, and you'll be the driver of the record car." Suddenly, his two jet cars looked a little archaic.

We 'three musketeers' had found our d'Artagnan to help us complete our speculative adventure. The intrepid four debuted at Union Grove Dragaway on September 5, with the *X-*

Chuck preparing for first ride in the X-1 sans body

1 ready to race, but without bodywork. Chuck piloted the *X-1* a few times that day, reaching 203.390 mph in 7.19s. In his maiden runs the car performed at a level equal to the best dragsters in the country. Chuck was hooked, shouting "Jets suck!"

The finally completed *X-1* ran exhibition dates at seven tracks in 1967. We were always concerned about safety before speed so the fuel tank emptied before the quarter mile, resulting in fantastic mid-6s elapsed times but low 200 mph speeds in the

Jake Schuljak checking out Chuck's preparation in early X-1 race

Completed X-1 ready for fun

timing traps as the car was already coasting down. Chuck provided more valuable information to put the finishing touches on the record-setting rocket racer.

Chuck and Ray looking over X-1

That winter a larger fuel tank was fitted and the fuel additive company, Rislone, provided a limited sponsorship for the *X-1*, dubbing it the *Rislone Rocket* in magazine ads. Rislone also had Chuck and Pete bring the *X-1* to the first Speed Equipment Manufacturers Association (SEMA) convention in Anaheim, California in January. Rislone arranged to get the car featured in Hot Rod, Car Craft, and Drag Racing magazines as well. Now Chuck and the *X-1* were national celebrities.

While in California, they took the *X-1* over to NHRA headquarters, asking Bernie Partridge and Wally Parks to consider allowing exhibition runs of the rocket car under their sanction. NHRA wasn't ready at that time to consider thrust cars on their tracks. The Rislone sponsorship fizzled later in the

Chuck preparing for another X-1 blast-off

summer when Bobby Unser won the Indy 500 in its sponsored Champ Car and the company exhausted its advertising funds promoting the unexpected victory.

Although Chuck and the *X-1* only had three race dates in 1968, the natural gas industry had been considering sponsoring our land speed record project proposal since late 1967. In July,

Reaction Dynamics was given $50,000 to begin working on *The Blue Flame*, with a promise of more to come if the gas industry could foresee the benefits of a successful result.

Chuck at the Oklahoma City 1968 jet and rocket race

Chuck's clean-cut appearance and easy manner

Natural gas industry executives checking out the X-1 at Oklahoma City

convinced the executives from the natural gas industry who had flown to Oklahoma City for the '1st Annual World Jet Nationals' in mid-September. He even wore a tie and dress shirt as he drove the *X-1* to over 265 mph and a 5.90s elapsed time. While the jet dragsters of Art Arfons, Doug Rose, J.D. Zink, and more were struggling to keep up, Chuck easily eclipsed their performances. The icing on the cake was Walt Arfons' steam rocket *Neptune*. The promoter wanted Chuck to match race Walt's car first. Because the steam car had a sketchy history, Chuck insisted they make a single pass first before running together. *Neptune* launched in a cloud of steam, veered off the track at the 1,000 ft mark and rolled over. End of match race.

When the jet cars refused to match race the *X-1*, the gas industry 'suits' were impressed at how easily the little rocket had defeated two former land speed record holders and agreed to raise the funds to complete *The Blue Flame*.

Walt Arfons steam rocket crashed before X-1 match race

Chuck elated after final run of theX-1 at Oklahoma City

Upon returning to our Milwaukee headquarters I was told by IGT that we should have our funding for *The Blue Flame* project in place before the end of the year, but we had to meet our original schedule to run it in 1969. I told Chuck he had to join us in our shop as soon as possible to help build the car, as we were staffing our Reaction Dynamics team to get the project on schedule. "I'll be there," was the response, "but you'll need to call my man, Gerard (Brennan), to help us build this thing."

Chuck's last celebration before fatal crash in piston-engine dragster

After the trouncing of the jet cars at Oklahoma City, confirmation that the land speed record project was being sponsored in whole by the natural gas industry, and the retirement of the *X-1,* made Chuck anxious about the prospect of waiting an entire year to feel the thrill of driving a fast car again. When a friend told him he needed help tuning his new Chrysler-powered dragster, he offered to accompany him to the 1968 Fall Championship at Rockford Dragway in Byron, Illinois. The speed demon beckoned Chuck once more.

Schuljak sadly commented: "How many guys got wasted hopping in someone else's car? In 1968 Chuck's dream, and also my dream, came to a halt. When that happened I lost all interest in racing. I had lost a partner, a friend that would never be replaced."

Howard Carpenter arrived at Rockford near the end of the day to watch the season finale. As Chuck prepared to hop in the dragster, Howard asked him what he was doing driving it. "I want to get my mind cleared up," was Chuck's response. "But, you're supposed to drive *The Blue Flame*!" Howard yelled back. He heard, "That's okay!" as Chuck put on his helmet and buckled into his narrow seat.

Howard then went down near the timing lights to watch him run. "He drifted left toward the edge of the track and dropped a wheel off the side - then he hit the timing lights, then an empty oil drum positioned alongside the pavement which virtually exploded into the rollcage, then hit the guardrail and began barrel-rolling." Running toward the wreck, Howard knew Chuck couldn't survive all that. Suddenly overcome with grief at the disaster before him, he sat down on the track, sobbing. When an approaching bystander asked if he was alright, Howard said sadly, "That was my best friend, and my partner."

"Well, no more," came the quiet reply.

Finally, we grieving three musketeers saluted our gallant fallen d'Artagnan in all of the nation's drag racing newspapers with a simple epitaph:

IN MEMORIAM

Charles M. (Chuck) Suba

April 23, 1938 – October 13, 1968

The Quickest – 5.90 sec. E.T.

The Fastest – 265.48 M.P.H.

-THE BEST-

-4-

DICK KELLER - FROM SPROCKETS TO ROCKETS

On July 23, 1966, a hot and sunny Wisconsin summer day, the space age came to motor racing. A revolutionary new dragster concept, the *X-1*, hurtled across the 1/4-mile pavement of Great Lakes Dragaway with a very excited and nervous driver at the controls. Three years' testing, two years' building, and a young lifetime of enthusiasm; this was the world's first successful rocket-powered race car. I was that driver.

Dick static testing the X-1 while chained down

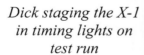

Dick staging the X-1 in timing lights on test run

79

I've been lucky, though I like to feel I made a lot of my own luck. Few men realize the acclaim and success in land speed record racing and motor sports design innovation. I was fortunate to be the designer of the first successful rocket-powered race car, the *X-1*; the project manager of Reaction Dynamics' successful *The Blue Flame* rocket-powered racer which streaked to the world land record speed of 630.388 mph; the designer and builder of the *Honda Hawk* motorcycle streamliner; and the rocket engineer, chassis consultant and designer for the *Pollution Packer* and *Pollution Packer Bonneville Dragster* race cars which set numerous national, international, and world records on the Bonneville Salt Flats.

How did this fascination with speed and rockets begin? As a boy, I saw a photograph of auto magnate Fritz von Opel's rocket car that had achieved a speed of 121 mph at Berlin's Avus track in 1928. Emblazoned on the car in large letters were the initials *RAK2*, a German abbreviation for the word 'raketen', or rocket, number two. My initials are RAK 3rd, and I imagined the coincidence to be Destiny pointing a finger at me. Thereafter, rocket propulsion and motor racing became my greatest interests and enjoyment.

Opel RAK2 which inspired the young Richard A. Keller (RAK3)

Racing car design was my boyhood passion. Laurence Pomeroy's 'The Grand Prix Car' was fascinating reading, with technical illustrations of historic European race cars from the earliest days into the 1950s. Later, I devoured the engineering lessons from Costin and Phipps' 'Racing and Sports Car Chassis Design'. When Mercedes-Benz debuted the highly advanced W196 Formula 1 car in 1954, along with the 300SL gullwing coupe engineering tour de force, I was overwhelmed with mechanical lust. Autographed glossy photos of Karl Kling, Stirling Moss, and the great Juan Manuel Fangio decorated my bedroom walls.

I seemed always to be in a hurry to get somewhere fast. I earned a reputation amongst my playmates in my Chicago neighborhood for modifying bicycles to go faster, stripping off excess weight and changing the sprockets for more speed. Using war surplus CO_2 cartridges for jet propulsion, I built (and wrecked) numerous balsa wood scale-model Bonneville lakesters.

The emotional stability of a close extended family gave me confidence to strive to excel in achieving my dreams. Growing up, we were a three-generation household with my maternal grandmother in residence. My paternal grandparents (and great-grandmother) lived a short walk away, on my route to school. The oldest of four siblings, I was handed new responsibility while in high school when Dad suddenly passed away at 41 years of age. This reality added a sense of urgency to my own life – to get on with reaching my goals.

While a teenager I built and drove 'hot rods' on Chicago streets and drag strips as a founding member of the Igniters Auto Club. Still in grammar school, my classmate Joe Hruban invited me to join him and a handful of friends to start the Igniters. In high school, we were often the butt of jokes, proudly wearing our club jackets, while not yet old enough to drive cars. But, we were a close-knit group and shared our mutual love for high performance automobiles, attending races and custom car shows. Then, in the late Fifties, I was further inspired when I became an occasional 'go-fer' for the greatest drag racing star of all time, Don 'Big Daddy' Garlits.

Dick's first stock car, partnered with Ted Garfield (KelGar)

1938 Chevy coupe with Corvette small block

B/Gas class Fordillac drag racer

Indy, Formula 1, and sports car racing were the epitome of auto racing in the 1950s, and I was an ardent follower of them all. Road & Track, Sports Car Graphic, and Hot Rod magazines littered my bedroom. In March, 1958, having arrived in Florida with spare tickets for the '12 Hours of Sebring' sports car race, I invited Don Garlits and his wife, Pat, to join me watching these exotic European endurance racers. We became good friends, and Don even bought himself an MG sports car afterward.

Garlits had a shop, 'Don's Garage', on Nebraska Avenue north of Tampa where he sold speed equipment, tuned and painted hotrods. It had originally been a gas and service station, probably built in the 1920s and sorely lacking paint. A room behind the service bay was his machine shop. Alongside his shiny new balancing machine stood an ancient lathe. Don had found it behind an old barn and had to cut down a tree grown between the ways to retrieve it. The compound rest carriage was missing some parts, so he hung a blacksmith's anvil from a chain below to keep it steady on the ways. He knew how to stretch a dollar.

Don wanted to show me his record-setting dragster, *'Swamp Rat'*, which was in the garage at his home a few blocks from the shop, on 122nd Avenue. As a student of race car design, I expected to see a neat chrome-moly spaced tube frame structure with all the latest aluminum and magnesium components. What a shock it was to see this homebuilt contraption using 1930 Chevy rails for a frame, the body held on with sheet metal screws, and a 5 gallon steel can for the fuel tank. At least it held a hemi engine, but with Stromberg carburetors instead of Hilborn fuel injection and 'weedburner' exhaust pipes with silver radiator paint instead of chrome. This was the fastest dragster in the world?

Dick in Don Garlits' first Swamp Rat dragster

The Swamp Rat posing with Dick on Garlits' Tampa front lawn

Pat and Don invited me to stay at their home and he spent the week explaining how his car worked. At this point I could see the genius in the man. He had a keen grasp of the mechanics and physics involved in extracting record-setting performance from his creation. He also has a firm grasp on his wallet.

Don Garlits became my mentor and inspiration over the next few years. Working occasionally as his pit crew man when time permitted gave me an education in engineering, and tenacity, that wasn't available in a classroom.

Art Arfons, left, looking on as Ed Garlits and Dick strap Don Garlits in the Swamp Rat dragster

85

He also made me a fan of drag racing.

Don Garlits and Setto Postoian discussing their next round at the 1958 ATAA championship drag race

Continuing my education after high school at Notre Dame University and Illinois Institute of Technology, my professional career has spanned fundamental and applied research as well as engineering design, development, and management. Early career highlights include research on aircraft boron fuels and silicone lubricants for the US Air Force, design of high vacuum test equipment used in developing new semi-conductor materials and integrated circuits, chemical warfare projectiles, military satellite defenses, NASA rocket-fueling monitors for the Saturn I and Saturn V Apollo booster rockets, and a study of the gas reaction kinetics of methane and oxygen.

Dick and the Saturn 1 Apollo booster in 1964 at Hunstville, Alabama Marshall Space Flight Center

The responsibilities of marriage and parenthood convinced me to rein in my speed lust from auto racing back to cycling, racing on the velodromes at Northbrook, IL and Kenosha, WI. Little did I realize the déjà vu that would follow later in my life.

Dick and his time-of-flight mass spectrometer at IGT investigating natural gas reaction kinetics

Experience gained at Phoenix Chemical Laboratory, IIT Research Institute, and the Institute of Gas Technology, in industrial and government contract research, led to me co-founding Reaction Dynamics, Inc. with Ray Dausman and Pete Farnsworth in 1965 to design, build, and develop new concepts in prototype and racing vehicles. Ray also worked at IIT Research Institute, and together we designed and developed the first hydrogen peroxide (H2O2) rocket motor for a racing car, the *X-1*. Its record-setting speeds on Midwestern drag strips eventually helped me to convince the

Racing at slower speeds on the Northbrook, Illinois velodrome

American Gas Association to sponsor what was to become a successful attempt on the world land speed record. On October 23, 1970, Long Beach native Gary Gabelich drove our rocket car, *The Blue Flame*, to a new FIA-recognized kilometer mark of 630.388 mph.

Getting The Blue Flame ready to launch

Yeah! We did it!

In 1971 at Reaction Dynamics, Pete and I designed and built the *Honda Hawk*, a turbocharged dual 750 cc 4-cylinder motorcycle-engine-powered land missile that zoomed across the Bonneville Salt Flats at 286 mph, more than 30 faster than the FIM world record at that time. Unfortunately, due to poor surface conditions that year, the required back-up run for the official record could not be made.

The Honda Hawk streamline motorcycle on the assembly beam

Dick, Jon McKibben, and Pete discussing the Hawk

Back on the Bonneville Salt Flats, on two wheels

*The Honda
Hawk ready to
go 286 miles
per hour*

After leaving Reaction Dynamics in 1972, I continued racing car design and building rocket propulsion systems as Keller Design Corporation. My engines have powered the *Pollution Packers*, *Miss STP*, *Conklin Comet*, and *American Dream* Rocket Dragsters, and the *Spirit of '76, Captain America, Moonshot, Chicago Patrol, Vanishing Point*, and *Natural High* rocket-powered Funny Cars.

Tony Fox's Pollution Packer rocket with the X-1 motor

Sammy Miller's first rocket funny car - Spirit of '76

*Keller Design KD-3500
production rocket motor
in Sammy's funny car*

*Lew Arrington sitting in his Captain America funny car with the
KD-3500 rocket*

Captain America blasts off at Union Grove, Wisconsin dragstrip

John Luna's Moonshot funny car with KD-3500 rocket

Fred Goeske's Chicago Patrol funny car with KD-3500 rocket

Sammy Miller's Vanishing Point chassis with KD-5000 rocket

Vanishing Point at the starting line

Larry Flickinger's Natural High with the KD-5000 rocket

The *Pollution Packer Bonneville Dragster*, a unique monocoque-chassis rocket-powered dragster, was designed by me and built by Tim Kolloch at R&B Automotive in Kenosha, WI. In addition to the world land speed record, my cars held, at the same time, all FIA standing start world acceleration and speed records up to one kilometer distance (see FIA Recognized International Record list). Numerous dragstrip records set coast-to-coast included the all-time NHRA low elapsed time (4.62s) and top speed (344 mph) for the 1/4-mile at an NHRA national event by Dave Anderson driving the *Pollution Packer* at the NHRA Summernationals in 1973, and the 1/8-mile (3.40s ET at 248 mph) in 1974.

*Tony Fox's Bonneville
Dragster setting
records on the salt flats*

Bonneville Dragster had 3 optional nozzles for thrust from 3500 to 7500 lb

Sammy Miller ultimately blasted his Keller Design-powered Rocket Funny Car, *Vanishing Point 2001/R*, to over 400 mph in 4.04s at Miami Speedway on December 3, 1977! I built powerful engines (!!!) and teamed with Tom Daniels at Race Car Engineering in Illinois to build the chassis. Sammy was a fearless driver. He drove the *Pollution Packer* dragster for Tony Fox for a while, and then ran my 3,500 lb

KD-5000 cast stainless steel production rocket motor

thrust rocket in his *Spirit of 76* funny car in 1975. That wasn't fast enough for Slammin' Sammy, so I launched a larger rocket motor line, 5,000 lb thrust and that 400 mph run was the result.

My competitive urges finally turned full circle when, as a Masters Category competitor, I returned to my early love, bicycle racing. I won several national track championships as well as setting European (UEC) and World (UCI) masters track cycling records.

World Masters racing at Manchester UK velodrome

Beginning with a young boy's fascination with sprocket technology, continuing through a young man's determination to excel, my quest for speed has certainly been rewarded with success. And driven by this philosophy: "Life is short; the road is long; ride fast!"

pursuit competition bike "Fear Maigh Eo" (Mayo man)
at Manchester UK

5-

IGNITING THE BLUE FLAME

Just after 11:15AM on October 23, 1970, an expectant group of mechanics, engineers and scientists watched with bated breath as a former astronaut stand-in clambered into a long pearlescent blue and white projectile, and prepared to take aim at the World Land Speed Record.

It was a cold and overcast day, and the threats of rain and the onset of winter were echoing there at the back of our minds. All the signs were that this would be our last chance in 1970 before the weather closed down our quest for the year. And probably forever!

At 11:20, *The Blue Flame* was on its way, and we waited anxiously until the speed report came through from USAC Chief Steward, Joe Petrali: an average of 617.602 mph through the flying mile. We were 17 mph over the existing record set five years earlier by Craig Breedlove; and now all we had to do was match that on the mandatory return run, within an hour of the first one. But that was easier said than done; twice already we had been in this position, and twice something heart-breaking had gone wrong. Our nerves were stretched taut.

Would today really be the day?

Many land speed record-seeking teams had found themselves in exactly the same position, but how did we come to stand on our threshold of history? How and why had *The Blue Flame* been built? Who built it? Where did they come from?

What dreams had driven on the innovative leaders of this project, and how did so many others come to share it?

These and many more questions are easily overlooked when public attention focuses on a handsome new hero and his feats. Just like a football team, where the running back does the shaving cream commercials on Monday while the 'grunts' that opened holes in the line on Sunday reside in anonymity, there was one Hell of a lot more human effort behind *The Blue Flame* than meets the eye.

So much had happened since Ray Dausman and I had started experimenting with our tiny rocket engine six years earlier. Chuck Suba, in our innovative *X-1* rocket-powered dragster, had destroyed dragstrip records everywhere in a two-year reign of speed superiority, as we sought elusive potential sponsors for our land speed record project. My position at the Institute of Gas Technology (IGT) in Chicago, a contract research and educational arm of the natural gas industry at the Illinois Institute of Technology (IIT), helped open the sponsors' doors. And in July of 1967 Dr Henry Linden, the Director of IGT, became our project champion and wrote to the American Gas Association (AGA) President suggesting we could get the job done with a $124,000 budget. This figure would ultimately prove optimistically low.

In early January, 1968, the management of Northern Illinois Gas Company (NIGAS) agreed to spearhead a drive to get financial backing from the entire American natural gas industry for our project. Their interest was spurred by our conceptual design of a liquefied natural gas-fuelled (LNG) rocket engine, which would power the big car. My original proposal outlined for the natural gas industry an 18-month design and construction program, intended to begin March 1, 1968, resulting in a subsonic world land speed record. The record attempt was projected for September, 1969 to exceed Breedlove's 600.601 mph. If this were successful, we would then make a supersonic - around 750 mph - record attempt the following year. NIGAS Chairman Marvin Chandler proposed an increased budget figure of $200,000 to the AGA. The number kept getting bigger as we learned more about our task.

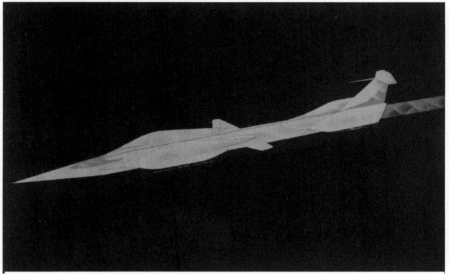

LSR artist concept for sponsor proposal

When we began building the *X-1* in 1965 Firestone and Goodyear were in a pitched battle, the 'tire wars', to become supreme in all the big-time racing venues; NASCAR, Indy cars, and drag racing. Both companies supplied LSR tires to the amateur racers at Southern California Timing Association's Bonneville Salt Flats racing events as well as the new jet car land speed racers. I drove to Akron, Ohio and met with Bill McCrary, Firestone's Manager of Race Tire Development, showed him my rocket test movie and asked for his support. He agreed to supply tires for our *X-1* and promised to keep us on his list for potential LSR sponsorship. This prospect would came to an end in November 1966 when Art Arfons crashed his *Green Monster* jet car at over 600 mph on the Bonneville Salt Flats during his last record attempt. Firestone eventually decided that possible negative publicity outweighed any benefit of further investment in that segment of motor sport. This was to become a serious blow to our ambitious project.

Later the following year I met with Jerry Tiffan who was the Goodyear Race Tire Development Group Product Manager. I had films of the *X-1* rocket dragster now as well as dragstrip results to back up my LSR proposal. Jerry said he would kick the project idea upstairs and get back to me. Initially, although Jerry had suggested Goodyear was interested, management decided otherwise. The competition with Firestone was slowing down and their racing budget was frozen. Besides, they already had the record, so why spend more money breaking it? At this point we saw our hopes of building our car dashed, with no tire company interest. However, the natural gas company executives were really enthused now and wanted this to happen. Jack Tankersley, President of East Ohio Gas Company, called Goodyear's President in Akron and laid it on the line. The natural gas industry, sponsoring *The Blue Flame* LSR project, purchased millions of dollars in tires and industrial equipment from Goodyear annually. It certainly would be a great incentive for Goodyear to support this very important American gas industry project.

Goodyear Tire & Rubber Company eventually agreed in late January, 1968 to supply the tires if a 700 mph maximum 'speed limit' was initially observed with our new car during the first year's record attempt. Since we were new to the land speed record game, they naturally wanted us to approach the record speeds with caution. Especially, the mysterious 'sound barrier'.

Initially, we had understood that the Goodyear Aerospace Division would consider joining with the tire division to provide wheels, disk brakes, cryogenic fuel tanks, titanium pressure vessels, drag parachutes, and an aerodynamic supersonic braking system using their parachute technology. Also, we were counting on Goodyear to fund the USAC timing costs as it had for earlier LSR attempts. But to our dismay Aerospace declined, so our once adequate budget was soon beginning to look insufficient.

The conservative natural gas industry comprising hundreds of independent gas producers, pipeline companies, and public utilities, did not immediately unite behind this exciting new project. Our intended March, 1968 starting date, therefore, came and went without a necessary industry-wide commitment for sponsor funding. At the end of May, Dr. Paul Torda and Dr. Carl Uzgiris, professors at IIT, were persuaded to begin consulting engineering work for Reaction Dynamics with assurance from IGT that our project would eventually be funded. Dr. Linden remained an enthusiastic supporter throughout the project and anted up the initial cash to prove it.

In August, 1968 Reaction Dynamics was advanced $10,000 of the requested funds from IGT if we would agree to build the land speed record vehicle in only 13 months, with a tentative commitment of $50,000 in all while the industry fund-raising for the balance continued. This could allow our original scheduled 1969 date to be met sometime during the three-month weather-limited late Summer/early Fall racing season at the Bonneville Salt Flats in Utah.

This was a major challenge, given our relative lack of experience working on this scale, but we set about dividing up the tasks for the project. Ray Dausman was assigned the responsibility of designing the propulsion system, assembling the components, and installing it in the vehicle. Pete Farnsworth would run the shop in Milwaukee and supervise the design of the vehicle's structure and its fabrication.

My job was to coordinate the aerodynamic design of the vehicle with consultants at IIT and Ohio State University, acquire associate sponsors and instrumentation for the record attempt, and press relations working with AGA's public relations firm Burson-Marsteller in New York City. Also, I drafted the detail design drawings for the chassis and rocket system. Later, I was responsible for designing and building the support vehicles; *The Blue Flame* trailer, hydrogen peroxide refueling truck, and the air compressor trailer alongside the race car in our little shop. Since we were contractually not allowed to place associate sponsor advertising on the car, I was only able to attract in-kind sponsors.

L to R, Dick Keller, Pete Farnsworth, and Ray Dausman in their
Milwaukee shop

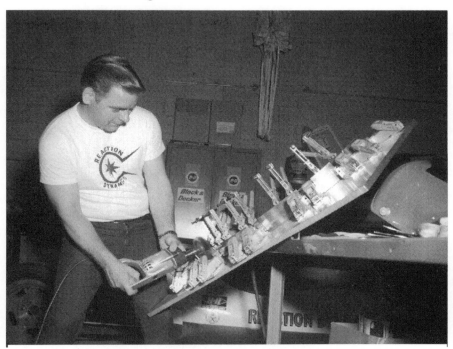

Pete building the welding fixture for the fuselage rings

Ray checking out the HP-LNG-22000-V rocket assembly

Dick examining the brass transonic wind tunnel model

Meanwhile, in mid-September, 1968, the *X-1* prototype had dominated that important jet car drag race at Oklahoma City. We had easily outsped two former land speed record holders, the Arfons brothers, Walt and Art, and set an astounding 5.90 second elapsed time record at over 265 mph. Representatives of natural gas industry companies who had witnessed the jet and rocket event were impressed and finally agreed to fully back the project with their cash sponsorship.

News Item: October 11, 1968 - Three astronauts were launched in the first manned flight of the NASA lunar spacecraft, Apollo 7.

With the initial finances finally secured, the project was again stalled when the nearly completed design had to be scrapped in October 1968, just prior to wind tunnel testing. The original version of the car was designed around Firestone's 28 inch diameter Bonneville tire used by Art Arfons' *Green Monster*. This in turn determined the cross-section area of the fuselage, drag coefficient, power requirement, and rocket engine fuel capacity. After Firestone quit LSR racing and Goodyear was persuaded to take on the tire supply, they determined that the time available would not permit adequate development of a new 28 inch tire, so the car would have to use a refinement of an earlier, proven 35 inch diameter design. Since our tire size had increased by 25%, the car grew geometrically in all dimensions – including cost. This would have major schedule repercussions that eventually led to us losing our car ownership through contract default.

The new design concept was finally completed in January, 1969 and sent to the Aeronautical and Astronautical Research

Laboratory (AARL) wind tunnel test facility at The Ohio State University in Columbus, Ohio. There, Paul Torda and his graduate student Tom Morel, collaborated with Dr John Lee, the AARL Director, on the tests and analysis of the results. In the laboratory, high-pressure air generated by huge compressors screamed through a 12 in x 12 inch transonic wind tunnel and over the instrumented

Dr. Torda adjusting the brass model in the Ohio State University transonic wind tunnel

brass model of *The Blue Flame*. Although our new design proposal had faired rear wheels mounted outboard on wing-like streamlined beams, the tunnel tests prompted a further redesign. Aft turbulence and ground plane interference in the transonic region were reduced by changing to open struts without wheel fairings.

*The Blue Flame model with wheel fairings before
wind tunnel tests*

The wind tunnel work was complicated and time-consuming and it soon became apparent that we needed a larger budget and more time. At the same time the fabrication cost for the necessarily larger rocket propulsion system had doubled. No new funds could be promised, so we took a deep breath and began working frantically to meet our rapidly approaching original schedule deadline.

The Blue Flame model with exposed wheels and struts after wind tunnel tests

Another challenge confronting us at this time was selecting a driver, which was still a terribly sensitive area with Pete, Ray and I after Chuck Suba's death the previous October. We contacted and screened more than a dozen candidates. Naturally, one of them was Craig Breedlove. If we hadn't talked with Craig, we'd eventually have to explain why to our sponsor.

I went out to see him in Torrance, California, because I knew the gas industry guys would ask about him. But even when we first began discussing potential driver names it was foreseen that, if Craig were to drive, it would be all about Craig since he had name recognition in the general public after all of his land speed record success, and not about the natural gas we wanted to publicize. I heard later that he mentioned a figure of $10,000 being offered to drive *The Blue Flame*, but I don't believe I ever got around to discussing money with him. And he had always been very heavily involved in the design of his own cars, so we weren't sure how all that could go down with us. After that pleasant interview in California, his name never came up again.

Since I knew Don Garlits quite well, after I had occasionally visited at his Florida home in the winter, and had crewed for him a few times, he was the top guy on my list. I also called famed drag racer Chris 'The Golden Greek' Karamesines in Chicago, since I knew all the Speed Sport shop guys at Blue Island, Illinois, but he really wasn't into the LSR idea. Doug Rose was from Milwaukee and Pete and I both knew him. He drove jets for Walt Arfons, and later his own *Green Mamba* jet car. The real negative for the gas industry was that Doug's legs had been severed below his knees in a jet dragster accident. The New York PR guys were concerned that if he was to have an accident in our car we would be criticized for putting a 'disabled' man in jeopardy in the car. They didn't know Doug! Don Beeman, who drove a jet car for Romeo Palamides, I believe, sent a resume as well, but Garlits had agreed by then, so we went with that choice.

'Big Daddy' was the perennial drag racing champion and expressed his interest in the new project, so I began negotiations with him for the ride. Although he was very well known in the drag racing community, he didn't have the national name recognition outside that genre, so that wasn't the problem it might have been with Craig.

Meanwhile Gary Gabelich, a drag racer from Long Beach, who had been involved in North American Aviation's astronaut training program, had approached us in Milwaukee in December about driving the retired *X-1* rocket car. None of us had the heart to race it again after the loss of Chuck, so we sold it to a Minneapolis snowmobile company, Sno-Pony. It was owned by Tony Fox who would later exhibit much interest in rocket-powered LSR cars. Fox modified the *X-1* for snow drags, while Gary went back home to Long Beach, California empty-handed.

Our little shop in Milwaukee finally swung into high gear in February, 1969 as the design firmed up. Fixtures were built, men hired, shop equipment installed, and construction of *The Blue Flame* finally began. Wind tunnel tests with the open, un-streamlined struts were meanwhile very encouraging. Construction continued, often outpacing the engineering efforts. We worked closely with our IIT engineering consultants who were desperately trying to keep a step ahead of Pete's time-pressed fabricators.

The Blue Flame project and driver Don Garlits were to be introduced to the public at a press conference on May 1, 1969 at the Beverly Hills Hotel in California. Two days before the

Don Garlits reviewing early design with Dick, Pete, and Ray at IIT

113

scheduled debut, Don regretfully withdrew as our land speed record vehicle driver due to family concerns and business obligations.

Don recalls: "I was looking forward to going out to Bonneville and going real fast. I'd never done that before and I thought it would be real fun. But my mother stopped the program. She was really good about intuition – she was like that, and could tell things before they happened. She said: 'In all your racing I've never asked you to do anything. I have a bad feeling about that – please don't drive that *Blue Flame* land speed car.' I respected her wishes and withdrew my driving deal."

Mrs. Garlits' premonition, as it turned out, was almost correct, it just involved the wrong car. On March 8, 1970, 10 months later, Don was driving his *Swamp Rat XIII* at Long Beach's Lions Dragstrip in the AHRA National Championships, when the clutch spectacularly exploded, cutting the car in half and amputating part of his right foot.

The scheduled press conference carried on with no driver being named at that time. Gabelich had made a good impression on his earlier visit to Reaction Dynamics that winter and so I contacted him the next day at his home in Long Beach. Meeting with him after the

Gary Gabelich with final version model of The Blue Flame

114

press party, he agreed to drive the new rocket car. On July 14 he began a series of six national press conferences for AGA, starting in Los Angeles, announcing his selection as *The Blue Flame*'s driver.

News Item: July 20, 1969 - Neil Armstrong and Edwin Aldrin exited the Apollo 11 lunar module and set foot on the Moon.

Meanwhile, back at Reaction Dynamics, things were no longer looking rosy. Our Milwaukee shop was burglarized while we were in California and we lost all of our new power and hand tools, which had to be replaced. Delays in receiving materials

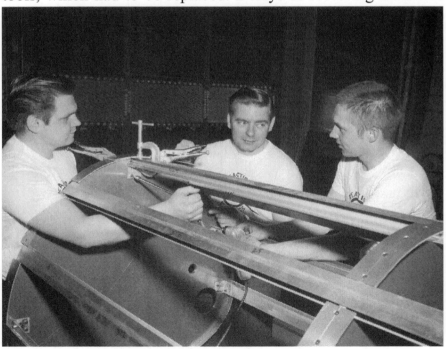

Mike McCarthy, Pete, and Dave Bykowski beginning inverted chassis assembly

and components slowed our progress considerably. In spite of taking on additional help and working 14 to 16 hours per day, the construction schedule kept slipping.

Our IIT consultants were frantically working on their design projects. However, although they did a remarkable job, the realities of working on a university's academic schedule resulted in delays in the transfer of their engineering output to our shop. We had to improvise quite often and hope our work would not be countermanded by the students' research and calculations. Our shop crew was becoming frustrated with their schedule. Dr Uzgiris and his students finally visited Reaction Dynamics for an update on the project. At this time the partially finished chassis was still mounted upside down on the H-beam we used as an assembly fixture. When they walked from our office into the shop they saw a large sign someone placed on the chassis:

'THE BEAM QUEEN – designed by more engineers than were necessary!'

After a few nervous smiles we got down to business and, remarkably, the engineering pace accelerated after that.

As Summer 1969 became Autumn the land speed record attempt was postponed twice, and finally abandoned for the year when winter rain inundated the salt flats, ending the year's brief racing season. Our workforce was reduced to a minimum as priorities shifted. By the end of January, 1970, the chassis was completed and on its wheels but funds for the actual record attempt were gone. Discouraged, Ray Dausman had left Reaction Dynamics and *The Blue Flame* to work for a Milwaukee engineering company.

*Pete, Dick, and Ray in front of the inverted chassis
assembly fixture before the aluminum skin was riveted*

*The Blue Flame monocoque chassis upright on the
assembly fixture after the bottom .040-inch thick
aluminum skin was riveted to the structure*

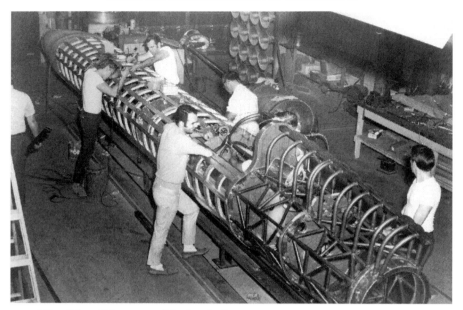

The Blue Flame welded tubular motor mounting structure in place on the assembly fixture

The Blue Flame monocoque .040-thick aluminum skin riveted and nose cone installed on the assembly fixture

The Blue Flame chassis finally on the ground with the rocket motor installed

The Blue Flame being prepared for finishing touches and paint

As if all this wasn't devastating enough, as a condition for us to continue the project, ownership of the car then switched from Reaction Dynamics to IGT under a revised contract. That was a crushing blow, after all the effort we had put in.

I no longer have a copy of the actual contract with IGT. But in general, the original agreement was for us to own, build and race *The Blue Flame* in 1969. AGA had invested a lot in publicizing the attempt for that year, and when we didn't get it done on schedule, we defaulted on the contract. Pete and I settled the default by turning over title of the car to IGT.

Ray had left Reaction Dynamics, and Pete and I were depressed for a while since the car had already been on its wheels, about 80% complete visually. We didn't believe we were totally at fault for the timing problems. We hadn't planned for this eventuality and were trying to come up with a new business plan in order to keep the shop and our own employment going. *The Blue Flame* was the only project we had.

We might have hoped that IGT would waive that clause, especially given the problems with budget which had delayed things through no fault of Reaction Dynamics, and then the Goodyear tire situation which changed the whole game plan again. We were not really experienced at negotiations of that sort and we had very little negotiating leverage. In the end Pete and I were really just motivated to be able to get the car finished and go for the land speed record.

Rightly or not, we also had a suspicion that IGT wanted to take the project over and cut us out now that *The Blue Flame* construction was almost done. It was briefly moved out of our shop as IGT exercised its newfound control, and down to Illinois for completion. This, of course, left us with an empty shop, no work there, and a long commute on the few occasions we were asked to go down to Illinois.

The IGT relocation of the car would soon backfire dramatically, however. While towing *The Blue Flame* on its trailer to a sponsor meeting at NIGAS in Aurora, Illinois, the IGT pick-up truck's driver spun out and left the rocket car and trailer overturned on the Dan Ryan Expressway. This made the local news and a *Chicago Tribune* photo story. I immediately sent copies of it to several AGA directors with a plea to get the car back in Milwaukee. IGT agreed, and thankfully we were once again back working in our own shop with a tight budget.

The Blue Flame being towed to a gas industry promotional meeting in Illinois overturned on its trailer on the interstate highway

News Item: April 13, 1970 - Apollo 13 suffered an explosion in mid-flight, aborting the lunar landing attempt.

The project continued under a low-cost profile through Winter and into Spring 1970 as Pete and I struggled to keep Reaction Dynamics' doors open and feed our families. On April 29 the shiny pearlescent blue fade-painted car was debuted at Astroworld Park in Houston during a convention of the Southern Gas Association member companies. This exhibition, with Gary Gabelich attending, renewed the gas industry enthusiasm for an LNG-fuelled record attempt. Additional funds were quickly generated through the continued efforts of Hank Harper of NIGAS and Dr Henry Linden of IGT, calling in favors and twisting arms. Once again *The Blue Flame* project forged ahead.

Pete continued detailing the chassis while I had taken over the rocket propulsion system responsibility. Ken McCarthy, our first full-time employee in 1968, worked with Farnsworth on the chassis while Gerard Brennan, an experienced race car builder and fabricator who had earlier completed most of the aluminum and steel structural welding, pitched in to assist me in finishing the installation of the rocket propulsion system and controls.

Dr. Henry Linden and Gary Gabelich at the Southern Gas Association meeting in Houston, Texas

Static tests on the rocket engine were scheduled for the end of July at Great Lakes Dragaway near Union Grove, Wisconsin and time was short. Mark Neubauer and Dave Bykowski, a fire fighter, worked evenings on the chassis and Larry Henkel moonlighted on the electronics. These men were to form the Reaction Dynamics land speed record crew at Bonneville. Additional part-time help included Dick Huebschen on the instrumentation, Dix Erickson, Roger Buetow, Harry Gunderson, Fred Butze, Larry Tanner, and Doug Bandl. Ray Besasie, an old-school metal craftsman, had earlier fabricated most of the aluminum compound shaped body panels for the nosecone and the cockpit.

Gerard Brennan watching Gary Gabelich during the initial static test of the rocket system at the Great Lakes Dragway in Wisconsin

On July 29, 1970 Gary Gabelich arrived in Wisconsin and we tied *The Blue Flame* to a strain gauge attached to a 9-in diameter steel post at the back of the dragstrip pit area to check the rocket engine's performance. Four days of testing and troubleshooting sent our team scurrying back to the Milwaukee shop to start on the changes we had determined were necessary. The thrust-measuring strain gauge was modified and recalibrated, the rocket engine inspected and fuel igniters added, weak spots reinforced, catalyst pack tightened up, and throttle mechanism modified.

Additional chassis detail updates were also completed.

Gerard Brennan static testing the rocket system in preparation for The Blue Flame's departure to the Bonneville Salt Flats

Testing resumed on September 2 with alternate driver Gerard Brennan at the controls. After three more days of development tests the rocket engine proved itself ready, the parachute deployment system was checked out and the vehicle was tow-tested to check the steering and brakes.

We briefly unloaded *The Blue Flame* in the shop for a final checkout. Our seven-man crew and part-time helpers worked their usual 16-plus hour days except for Sundays (only eight hours!) until the car left for the western Utah desert on September 12. Exhausted, we still caravanned straight through to Utah, alert with excited anticipation of what lay ahead, arriving in Wendover and unloaded the car on the salt the next morning on Monday, September 14. Finally we were ready to take our shot at that ultimate prize – the world land speed record.

-6-

BOB ROSENBERG – SELLING THE FLAME

Bob Rosenberg was the man who sold *The Blue Flame* deal to Henry Linden of IGT, and was thus the guy who really set the ball rolling.

"Well, Dick Keller was a technician who worked for me at the time at IGT and our laboratory was down in the basement. One day in conversation he was talking about the work they were doing on the *X-1*, the dragster, and that went on for a couple of days. He was talking then of doing a world land speed record but the dragster wasn't capable of doing it, obviously, and in addition the hydrogen peroxide rocket by itself wasn't capable of doing it. So one thing led to another, and the idea of using natural gas then as the additional energy boost germinated in our discussions.

"We were kinda sparking off each other, and I can't remember whose idea it was. It was like 'Oh, why don't we use natural gas?' kind of thing. 'Yeah, let's look into that. Gee, the exhaust is hot, it's got oxygen, so why not?'

"At that point then I conceived the idea of, 'Hey, maybe we can sell this to the gas industry and use it as a publicity thing. Natural gas has always been seen as stodgy, an old folks' thing…' It was a very big sell. One of my favorite stories is that we got a letter back from the then president-chairman, of the biggest gas company in the United States, which essentially said that if man was meant to go that fast God would have given him wheels. That was the mindset of the industry at that time."

Bob had seen the *X-1* in action before he approached Henry, and liked what he saw.

"I didn't realize that Dick had any racing background at all, I didn't know the other guys. He had some pictures of the car. Recently we disagreed where I first saw it. He says Oklahoma City, but I think it was an Iowa dragstrip. He may be right! But my recollection of it is that it was the first time I ever saw the car when they were running against Art Arfons in the *Green Monster* in an exhibition in Iowa. Art's car came up, guys were pushing the thing, the engine was roaring, then there was a bigger fire when he kicks in the afterburner. Then the *X-1* drives up by itself, not six guys pushing the car. They get up to the line, ready to stage, then the afterburner comes on and the flames are coming out the back of Arfons' car. There was a wire fence behind it, and a cornfield. And the corn went down. This roar of the *Green Monster* starts and then the *X-1* goes *whee* – and beats

Pete Farnsworth explaining the X-1 rocket dragster to the natural gas industry executives at the Oklahoma City drag strip in August 1968

the hell out of it! It was an amazing experience to see that. You're just decomposing a chemical, and it's shooting out the back end, action and reaction.

"So then I had to get approval because this was not exactly research within the mission or what IGT normally did. My direct boss was a man by the name of Jack Heubler, so I needed Jack's approval even to carry it through to Henry Linden and then try to convince Henry that we should try to go out and put the IGT stamp of approval on this thing. I got Jack's approval, then Henry essentially said, 'Okay, if you can pull it off, I'll support it.' He backed that up and put some letters together for us, using his name. He was absolutely necessary, without his imprimatur I don't think we would have pulled it off. But just his imprimatur wasn't enough. We needed a gas industry hero, supporter, whatever the right term for that is, we needed a leader within the industry to take that on. And that became Northern Illinois Gas, or NI-Gas.

"What happened was that we pitched it to AGA, and the president of AGA then said, 'Okay, you can talk to the advertising/PR committee, and that was where the public relations director Hank Harper decided hey, this looked pretty exciting, and he got their president, Joe Gauthier, involved. Joe's imprimatur was the one that we really needed and he did some personal phone calls and some arm twisting. It was his leadership that really put it over the top."

Rosenberg oversaw the build of *The Blue Flame*, at Reaction Dynamics' workshop in Milwaukee, and was impressed by the workmanship he saw there. But to this day he has his enthusiasm for Goodyear under firm control, remembering the effect the change in tire specification had back in 1969.

"Goodyear was a problem from Day One. Getting tires out of them. They didn't wanna do it, then they dragged their feet, then they changed the specs. They were really bad."

He ran the project, until he was replaced by Dean Dietrich late in 1969 at Henry Linden's behest.

"I was a technician, kind of a boffin, I guess you could say, and was running it through most of the construction phase, until that was pretty much squared around. I got Paul Torda of IIT involved, who got the rest of that crew together. I had been working with him in an organization called the Combustion Institute, so I knew his background, experience and expertise and he was a guy I trusted. So I talked to him about what he could do. I'm a combustion guy so I was moving into an area I didn't have a lot of expertise in. So Paul agreed to be the consultant on it for me, and he got Carl Uzgiris and Tom Morel involved and then built that whole chain. It gave us a specialist expertise that IGT just didn't have in-house. Without that we couldn't build an engine big enough, so that was a crucial element."

Besides the effect of Goodyear's change in tire size, the other major drama was the famed crash on the Stevenson Expressway. "Only the hard shoulder was open as the car and its trailer had blocked all the other lanes. That really was one of those, 'Oh, my God!' moments when we first heard about it. We were running out of money, we were very, very tight on it. And if the car had been damaged, we were dead, it was all over. We were so lucky that it didn't have a scratch on it!

"When we took it to Bonneville, I was out there with the first wave when we were first setting up out there. I was there for the run that Gary made, when he got stuck out on the salt. He had kept talking about the soft salt and Don Fleming and I, being great researchers, we didn't quite know what he was talking about. So after he got stuck and had to get pulled out we drove our car out there and also got stuck. Broke right through the surface. We had to walk all the way back to the crew's trailer and everyone was gone at that point, so we had another long hike, getting cold out in the desert. It's an amazing place. Other than the highway you could see, you could be in the middle of no place."

While Bob loved The Blue Flame, he admits that he wasn't entirely convinced about its colorful, long-haired driver.

"Gary was... strange is the word, I guess. Physically he was quite a specimen, and his reflexes obviously worked okay, but he was quieter than I expected him to be. When he did talk he was kinda strange. He was always like a hippie, very much so. I never got a lot of confidence in Gary, he always bothered me a bit. He was always a question mark to me. All of his credentials said he had the capability to do it, but he wasn't conventional, not at all! Certainly not the kind of guy that Pete and Dick and the rest of the crew were; they were much more solid straight shooters, dedicated kind of people. Gary didn't fit that mold. There was the story of him throwing firecrackers into a can of nitromethane, that kind of thing, that seemed to fit the personality.

"But he got the job done. I remember he always kept saying he wanted to drive towards the Floating Mountain first, in case anything went wrong, because going the other way the next opportunity is the ditch before he hit the highway.

"So much of *The Blue Flame* was right first time. But the one thing when we got out to the Salt Flats that we suddenly decided that we didn't have was an American flag decal. And my big contribution to the time out there was running around Salt Lake City trying to find an American flag decal! I found two, and we had them on either side of the tail fin.

"I wasn't there when they set the record. Joe Gauthier was on a cruise at the time and he was very concerned whether we were going to be successful as he had put a lot of prestige in this thing. He was calling almost daily to find out what was going on. Almost? He *was* calling daily! When the word came down that they were going to make the last try and I told Joe, and then we found out that they had actually done it after Don Fleming had called me with the news, it was *'way*! Now I could tell Joe we actually did it! So I called him, after I'd driven into Wendover. The phone book was one eight and a half by eleven piece of paper. He was elated and relieved!"

Bob's involvement with *The Blue Flame* ended with the successful record run.

"Joe kind of lost interest, so we lost our gas industry champion. They were having some money problems, so I talked to them and talked to IGT, but we just couldn't find another money source in order to keep it going. I believe we were looking for another $175,000 at the time, for 1971.

"We expected just the opposite of what happened. Hey, we proved we could do it; we got this other program, now we can really get more publicity! And it went the other direction. Maybe had Joe not been out on a cruise, maybe had he been in Chicago, had he gone to the Salt Flats to see things and actually been out there, who knows what? And of course the delays didn't help us either; there became a lot of uncertainty, a lot of angst. Once we had the car out there, I think people in the gas industry felt it should have been like your family sedan, you turn the key, you drive it there, you drive it back, it's all done.

"The trouble is, you can't go in full of negative possibilities and sell it like that. You cannot tell a sponsor all the problems. In part, you don't *know* all the problems, because there are gonna be things, like burning the parachutes. You never woulda guessed we'd have a problem with that. One of the vivid memories was when Gary deployed the first chute and it burned off, and they were hollering on the radio: 'Don't deploy the second one!' and he had already pulled it and burned it off too and he kept right on going. Never woulda guessed that kind of problem.

"My biggest disappointment was that our program was always a three-year one. Our first one was to beat the land speed record. The second one was the speed of sound. And the third one was to go 1000 mph on the ground. The car absolutely woulda done it. There is no doubt in my mind.

"That was a real shame, that it never happened that way. We were neophytes, nobody really knew us by that first run, so we didn't really get the publicity you would have got on a second attempt. We had now proved ourselves, we'd been out there and done the job…

"Carl Uzgiris felt that IIT benefited a lot from their involvement. The gas industry benefited some from the project, sure, but nowhere near as much as they could have because they didn't exploit what they had afterwards. The project was aimed at young people and we should have been pushing this down through the schools, at that level of person, and we never really did that. IGT wasn't geared for it but AGA should have been the entity to do it and never really picked it up. So no, I don't think at all that they got what they shoulda got out of it. Half a million dollars was a lot of money, so it was quite a sizeable project, but it was real, the success was real. At IGT we were doing everything from trying to make self-cleaning ovens to trying to improve industrial processes, and while the research might have been a success, we couldn't commercialize it or quantify it. But *The Blue Flame* was real, it was hard, it was there, other people recognized it. It went into a record book. So it was a very, very great success.

"Did it help my career? Now that's an interesting question. I was going to answer that immediately 'No,' and then I've got to take that back a bit. Technically and professionally, it really had no impact. What it did do was get me exposure to the upper echelon, the Joe Gauthiers, the presidents of companies that I think I would have gotten ultimately because that was my personality and my direction. But I remember while we were still trying to raise the money AGA had an executive conference in Hawaii and Joe asked me to come there and talk to a bunch of the people - executive level, chairmen - to try to convince them to put money into the project. So I met a lot of people that I wouldn't have met in ordinary circumstances.

"Joe and I ended up getting drunk on his patio with Gracie, his wife, because enough people had ended up saying yes that we were pretty sure we were over the top with it. So I would have to say yes, from that point of view. It got me exposure and contacts and people remembered my name as a result of it.

"On a personal level, I still feel good about it. For me it was a step up, it wasn't what we normally did at IGT. It was something very different and I was out of my element. I still had all my other responsibilities which I had to oversee and write my reports for and so forth, so it was very much a sideline. But to pull it off was so fulfilling and I still feel good about it, about being involved with the last American car to hold the land speed record. It was beautiful, a gorgeous thing. I still keep two models of it on my mantelpiece."

-7-

TOM MOREL – AERODYNAMIC GENIUS

"When I came to the Illinois Institute of Technology in January 1968 I found out that the scholarship I had come for wasn't going to happen after all. I was promised it but when I got here to the United States the guy that had promised it just said, 'What scholarship?' So I didn't have too many choices. I had about five bucks in my pocket, and no idea what I was going to do.

"The chairman of the IIT Armour College of Engineering's Department of Mechanical, Materials and Aerospace (MMAE) department, Professor Andrew Fejer, was a Hungarian who had married a Czech lady and I came from Czechoslovakia so I think he took pity on me! He gave me a job and we were just moving the department from one building to another so he gave me some menial tasks to build the furniture and so on, I got paid a little bit. After a while I did some drafting for him as he was writing a book, and it took about two months like this and I was getting a little bit of money to get by and he gave me a loan, but it was not enough. Then he talked to his friend who was also Hungarian, Dr Paul Torda. He was an aeronautics guy, a professor in the MMAE department, and he started to fight for me, but I had no background in aerodynamics, no courses, no nothing. But Torda said, 'Oh, I'll give you a chance. No problem.'

"So I got together with Torda and he had this project. He had just at that moment been approached to help with *The Blue Flame*. He worked sometimes for the Institute of Gas

135

Technology as a consultant and knew Bob Rosenberg. They had gone to him as an aerodynamical expert, to take on that part of the task. And they went to Dr Carl Uzgiris to do the mechanical part. So they formed two teams and Carl had like five students and Paul had just me because it was a much smaller project. But more interesting to me!

"Paul asked me before he told me what the project was whether I wanted some support and I said, 'Sure, I wouldn't mind more support. What's the project?' And then he told me. And I said, 'I can't do that. I have no idea what you're talking about! I have never taken a fluid mechanics course in my life, I have no clue!' And he said, 'That's no problem, here are some books.' And he gave me a stack of books and said, 'Go read them and come and talk to me when you come to something you don't understand.' So I said, 'Fine.'

"Huh! So I started to study this stack and the first thing I did then was to take some courses in fluid mechanics. So I read books, I went to classes and I talked to Paul. We would have these meetings and I would come in and I would say 'I don't really know where we would start.' And he would say, 'No problem.' And at that time he had an idea how you would go about it and he had a stack of reports from NACA, the National Advisory Committee for Aeronautics, which was the forerunner of NASA, the National Aeronautics and Space Administration. These guys had produced the underpinnings for mostly military aircraft and rockets. Paul had a section that was declassified, reports from China Lake out in California where they had developed rockets in the desert. What they had was a kind of railroad arrangement, with rocket sleds on it.

"A lot of the reports had to do with the design of the under shape, so I studied that, and the problem they had was lift. That was one of the biggest concerns I had throughout this project until they stopped running the car, that it was going to lift off. I didn't want to kill the guy. Once you take off you come down hard and crash, at these huge speeds.

"A lot of the things that I learned in this process were from these NACA reports. And Paul gave me some other books. He didn't read them all but he had an understanding of what the formation must be. He never really studied it with me, but I would come and show things to him and he would explain to me some important point. He was pretty hands-off, but he would guide me invisibly in the right direction and to the right information.

"There were a couple of things I picked up, and one of them was the nose shape. That came from these reports. Some of them recommended this, some recommended that, some talked mostly about cones, but what seemed to be most convincing to me at the time, reading from these reports, was an ogival shape.

"The other thing was the ground effect, which we were concerned about. That's why the car had that somewhat triangular construction of the fuselage. That was to alleviate the pressure build-up, if the shockwave bounced up off the ground.

"The last thing we obsessed over was how much negative angle to give the car. We didn't want to do too much from the point of view of drag, but enough to keep it down. We didn't want to overdo it because we weren't sure about the tires.

"Then of course we had to work with Dick Keller and Pete Farnsworth over things like the size of the tanks that they wanted to put into the car. That's why we ended up with such a long car, thirty-eight and a half feet, by the time we had all the tanks in and room for a driver."

Like Craig Breedlove, with *Spirit of America – Sonic 1*, Tom says he looked at the coke bottle shape, but was not impressed. "It was to do with the area rule on airplanes, and took into account the wings, but his car didn't have any wings so I don't think it was doing a thing for him. I'm not sure he knew what he was doing with that, necessarily; he had seen something and was doing it by the seat of the pants… That's why we came up with a straight-sided, ogival cylinder shape.

"We built two different scale models and tested them in wind tunnel models, and that was fun for me because I was exposed to some wonderful things. Torda used his connections and knew somebody in Wichita, and we tested in the tunnel at Wichita State University there and got some of the design validated. The first model was six-foot-long, the other one a foot long, 1:25 scale.

"After those first tests we still had the issue of primarily what happens when it goes through the speed of sound, because the design was supposed to be supersonic - what speed it would kick in, whether there would some drag rise, and lift. So we paid a lot of attention to the smaller model and the drag was really taking off around that speed. After the conclusion of the second tests, which were supervised by Dr John Lee, the director of the Transonic Wind

IIT graduate student Tom Morel and Dr. Paul Torda examining the Ohio State University transonic wind tunnel and test model

Tunnel Laboratory at the Ohio State University in Columbus, we decided the design was fine in respect of the drag and lift characteristics at speeds up to Mach 1.10 and we didn't change it after that.

"Initially we had covers on the outrigger rear wheels and I wanted to have an aerofoil section to cover the struts that attached them to the chassis, because we got so scared about lift. We never used the wheel covers for structural reasons and it must have been a cost item for the airfoils because we never had them or the pressure sensors I'd wanted. The rear fin was the size it was for safety, to keep the car running straight, because we wanted a stable car that was self-stabilizing. It only had a degree or so of steering, just to keep it running straight.

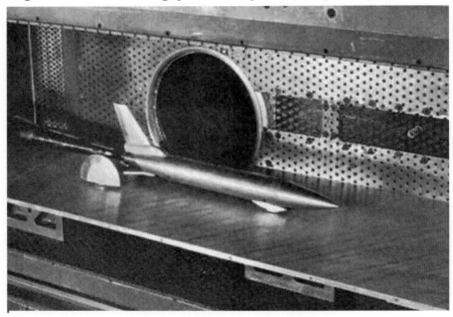

First test model version of The Blue Flame with wheel fairings on the wind tunnel

"A lot of the process of putting it all together was interesting, and a lot of it was done by the guys themselves. Pete and Gerard Brennan did all the welding and a lot of the fabricating. Aluminum welding, pretty sophisticated stuff. The last thing I did on this project was to instrument it, to be able to measure some pressure distributions. But I think by the time they actually got the record nobody cared about all that anymore, and by then I was already deep into my other studies."

Tom wasn't present when Gary Gabelich broke the record in the car he had shaped.

"I was there for some of the trials and then I had to go back to school. After I left they started again, so I wasn't present when it happened.

"I think what they needed was more power. There was one big blow along the way when it became obvious the power would be much, much lower than they had originally counted. And the drag rose dramatically at Mach 0.8.

"But what I saw was awesome, truly awesome. You would be standing about a hundred yards back, and it was about four and a half miles run up to the measured distance and the same to slow down. When you were out there and the car was at the end of a run, you barely saw it. It was very far. And on a warm day on the salt flats there is a kind of haze and you don't see clearly. You see like a mirage. The air shimmers. And then out of that shimmer you got an apparition, you see something glisten. You don't really hear much, but eventually you hear the noise when it goes by. It was awesome!

"But you know, the funny thing? Since there was this lack of interest from the gas industry I didn't really get excited when they broke the record. I was happy for them, mostly happy for Dick and Pete, but it didn't leave that much impression. It was mostly my friends in Europe who got excited by it, sending me clippings. It was almost a non-event here, there was nothing in the U.S. One time they ran a full-page advertisement, but that was it."

The story was that Gary asked Goodyear for $1,000,000, having heard that was what it had paid Craig. But Craig's money was spread over all the years of his projects and included the cost of building two cars. When Gary refused to sign a contract, Goodyear excluded him from all its advertising regarding *The Blue Flame*.

"Gary was a very good-looking guy. He was perfect for it! A very attractive guy. He was brave and skilful, sharp reflexes. He was very good, but talking to him he didn't seem very smart. I really liked him. A funny story: there was a TV guide from a newspaper once and on the cover was a picture of me with Paul Torda and *The Blue Flame* and the caption described me as Gary Gabelich. They had no clue! That was my moment in the sun. If they called me Gary Gabelich, I'd take it. It could have been worse!

"I was told that after they had broken the record he went into the Stateline Casino, which was the only one in Wendover back then, and went up to this big machine and started playing it, and then hit the jackpot! That's what I was told…

"The other story is that the next day they woke up after setting the record, and it had snowed…"

Tom Morel was 25 years old when he graduated as an MS in Mechanical Engineering in 1969, and not long out of Czechoslovakia. A young man now living in a big new world. Wasn't he just a teensy bit daunted by the fact that he had been tasked almost immediately with designing the shape of a supersonic car when, by his own admission, he didn't really know anything about fluid dynamics?

"No, not really. But it's funny, most of my friends don't know anything about this. I just don't talk about it. I've never been really awed by it. I just happened to kind of come along when the real heroes like Dick and Pete and the rest of them had this vision and passion. I never felt that it was something to play up in my background, or important. I thought I was just a lucky guy at the right moment when something interesting was going on. I just stumbled into this, because I didn't have any money. You see how great it is not to have any? I never truly looked at this as the most important thing I've ever done. This is not up there, at all!"

After *The Blue Flame* project he worked at IIT on structural design for special machinery, a total change of direction and because he needed money. "Sometimes things work out! That's Fate, I guess. I guess I was fated to do *The Blue Flame* project. And to get on a magazine cover, under a different name, there by mistake!

"But I was pleased to have the opportunity to be around these guys. They were cool, such great guys. Dick was the face of the team. He did all the speaking and the cheerleading, and I'm sure his enthusiasm was very important in securing the money. Pete was a quiet guy who didn't say much and always looked serious, not like a jokester or anything like that. But they were like twins. And I thought that Carl Uzgiris did a really good job on it too. These guys were heroes, Dick and Pete, and the others."

But though Tom Morel would probably, in his self-effacing way, still be the first to deny it, he was one too…

142

-8-

CARL UZGIRIS – MECHANICAL WIZARD

Dr Sarunas 'Carl' Uzgiris was the man tasked with turning the basic concept of *The Blue Flame* into safe and reliable mechanical hardware.

"I was born in Lithuania during the war and ended up in Germany, but in 1950 my family emigrated to the USA and settled in Springfield, Illinois. Since Lithuania had ceased to exist we had no passports, so I was effectively a 'man without a country.'

"I received a BS in Mechanical Engineering from the University of Illinois, an MS in Mechanical Engineering and a PhD in Mechanical and Aerospace Engineering from the Illinois Institute of Technology in 1966 and joined the faculty as an assistant professor.

"My academic interests were in the area of structures and dynamics - Paul Torda's expertise was aerodynamics. So when Paul was approached by IGT about this project he realized that I might be interested in handling the chassis design. The project seemed interesting, with novel design problems and some serious backing via IGT. Also, at the time I was in a position to involve several graduate students who were interested in working on research projects at the Master's degree level. The project had sufficiently challenging problems to satisfy that need."

Among them were Krishna Pandey, Shashikumar Kurani, Manoj Adhikari, Harshad Parikh and Prahlad Thakur.

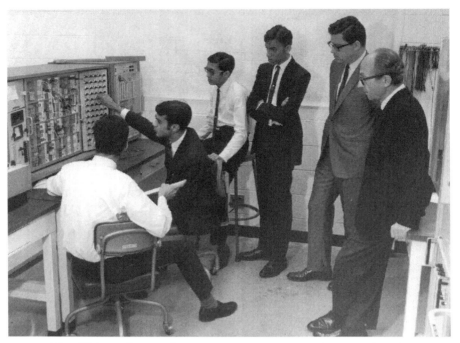

The IIT mechanical engineering team working under the direction of Dr. Carl Uzgiris and Dr. Paul Torda at the right

"The project was ideal for involving such people. It needed lots of enthusiastic and cheap engineering labor - hence graduate engineering students. I lost track of my students that worked on the project. But I'm sure that they still remember it as a pleasant experience. Five of them who worked on it used it in partial satisfaction of the requirements towards their Master's degrees in Mechanical Engineering."

Dick Keller reflects: "Looking back at the work Dr Uzgiris and his Indian charges contributed to *The Blue Flame* project, it is quite a remarkable achievement. As a young assistant professor, Dr Uzgiris' peers suggested this project would damage his career as nothing would come from it. Paul Torda convinced him to take the opportunity. And one has to understand the limitations of working within a university engineering curriculum environment. These young men were, first of all, students who needed to maintain high grade point averages to remain in the graduate program. Also, they were working within a semester system that affected their work schedule, not in a good way for our project.

"Pete Farnsworth and I were under a lot of pressure to meet our project schedule commitment. Due to the nature of these things, funding came later than we had anticipated, and this delayed the start of IIT's engineering contribution. As a result, we were continually pressuring the IIT group to hurry up and give us the information we needed to construct the vehicle. Dr Uzgiris understood this, too, and kept the communication between our teams open and current.

"My experience at IIT Research Institute with Indian students before this was not encouraging, either. Most Indian graduate students were from the privileged class back home, with little or no life experience of things mechanical. They were excellent theoreticians, but not practical. These young men were exceptional as it turned out. I believe Carl's mentoring was in large part responsible for their successful work.

"Realizing our urgent plight to keep construction moving along, the IIT team worked many long hours with great enthusiasm. We met frequently, sharing our racing and fabricating knowledge with the engineering input from the lads. In retrospect, I still find it amazing that we had absolutely no mechanical problems with *The Blue Flame* throughout the project. Remember, all of this engineering and design work was done with paper, pencils, and slide rules.

"Dr Harshad Parikh has had a career as patent examiner at the U.S. Patent Office. He related that throughout his career, *The Blue Flame* project has stirred the most interest from readers of his resume. Prahlad Thakur, Manoj Adhikari, and Krishna Pandey remained in the United States with successful engineering careers. Shashikumar Kurani returned to work in his native country, India."

"I had no background or particular interest in racing," Uzgiris continues. "However this vehicle was beyond what one normally thinks of as a racing vehicle. Thus background knowledge of racing vehicles was not an issue. Besides, at that stage of my career I had no fear of novelty or failure.

"I presumed total design freedom - within reasonable financial and time constraints - and got it. Otherwise I would not have embarked on this adventure."

Uzgiris remembers that many people had inputs to *The Blue Flame's* basic 'tricycle' configuration. "And, ultimately, when you consider the requirements posed by the engine/fuel system, the aerodynamics, the structural dynamics and stability, the semi-monocoque structure becomes inevitable.

"The central portion of the vehicle was a ring and stringer construction with riveted skin panels sub-divided by bulkheads. Since the fuel tanks were mounted in this part of the vehicle, such a structure permitted maximum volume for a given length and cross-sectional area. Furthermore, this construction allowed the vehicle skin to be used in a load-carrying capacity, thus minimizing the weight of the chassis. The fuselage materials were aluminum. To ensure against panel buckling and flutter at extreme loads, skin panel areas were kept below a maximum of 10 by 10 in.

"The ogive-shaped nose cone was an aluminum monocoque shell with a fiberglass sandwich lining and was supported by an internal welded-steel structure attached to the front bulkhead. The high-pressure air and helium tanks used for pumping the fuel were mounted in this structure.

L to R, Dr. Uzgiris and Pete Farnsworth discuss the monocoque chassis bulkhead design with IIT graduate students Harshad Parikh and Manoj Adhikari

"The rear of the vehicle carried the engine, wheel struts, tail fin and braking chutes and was thus subject to high loads, so semi-monocoque construction was not suitable and instead a welded nickel steel tube frame was employed.

"The wheel layout and the suspension and steering system were dictated by aerodynamics and stability constraints, again with many contributors to the final configuration.

"The front of the vehicle was suspended on a coil spring and a dashpot suspension, while at the rear we didn't use suspension as the tires acted as the shock isolator. The front wheels steered with a ratio of 90 to 1.

"The wheel assemblies were spin-tested up to 850 mph and were expected to perform satisfactorily on the vehicle at 750 mph."

Bob Rosenberg firmly believed that without getting IIT involved, with its specialist expertise that IGT just didn't have in-house, they wouldn't have been able to build the big version of the rocket motor, but Uzgiris points out that he himself had very little involvement on that side, "Other than general oversight involvement.

"IGT was involved as an overall project manager from the point of view of finance, recruitment, PR, etc. IIT had overall technical responsibility. The really heavy lifting was done by Keller, Farnsworth et al. They were the real originators of the concept and ultimately made the project work.

"Tom Morel and Paul Torda did some pretty novel aerodynamic science. Their contribution was also key to making it all work and, in particular, made the outcome predictable. Finance was certainly tight, but fortunately the project was blessed with lots of 'slave' labor."

He was also a firm believer in Gary Gabelich and praised his contribution. "Gary was perfect. We needed his dedication and risk-taking ability. The man had no fear. I attended some of the tests at Bonneville, and admit that I lost some sleep over it.

"Not reaching supersonic speed was a bit of a let-down. Nonetheless a novel record was set. But I am rather pragmatic about it. Nothing in life is ever 100%. The project led to a sense of accomplishment and satisfaction. Produced some publications and presentations. Added a bit of zip to my CV.

"Looking back four decades later, on the last American car to hold the land speed record, it was a privilege to work with a great bunch of guys - a unique combination of dedication and persistence on the part of Dick Keller, Pete Farnsworth et al."

-9-

DEAN DIETRICH – KEEPER OF THE FLAME

Dean Dietrich was the man who played the crucial role of taking over the running of the project and making the finances make sense.

"I ran the business end of the Institute of Gas Technology, the people sponsoring it. So I knew about the project from the time it started. At that time it was just another project that I kept track of, all the finances. I could see where it was going along the way. Like most racing things, that meant 100 percent behind the timescale and 100 percent over budget! But it's always hard to figure out something like this. You can't point blame at anyone, that's just the way these projects go.

"One morning the president of the company, Henry Linden, needed a ride to work so I picked him up and on the way he was telling me how distraught he was about the project. He was the big prime mover behind it, the man who went out and raised the money in the first place.

"At that time I was doing a little gymkhana with Corvettes and was into racing, and so I said, 'Well, Henry, I know a little bit about racing and how to run a business; if you need any help just let me know.' He says okay. So I drop him off at the office, I park my car, get into my office and my secretary says, 'Henry would like to see you.'

"So I went in and here was sitting Bob Rosenberg, who was the current project manager. And Henry looks at Bob and says, 'Starting now, Dean's the project manager, you're off the project. Don't worry about it any more.' So that was how I ended up with the project. Bob was the technical guy, I was financial.

"But don't take away from Bob, because he had done a great technical job. It was pretty much done but we were out of money and had to raise more, hence the need for me. I had the guys from the United States Auto Club (USAC), who were going to do the timing for the record run, go up and take a look at the car. We were supposed to go to the Flats in September or October 1969, and one of these guys called me up and said, 'That car won't be done maybe until a year from September.' That kind of threw the red flag up.

"So I started spending two days a week going up to Milwaukee, as well as doing my regular job, to kind of get my arms around it and get it going again. Get them on budget and raise some money."

Dietrich slipped easily into his potentially tricky new role, minimizing any friction with all of the parties concerned. "I don't remember anything untold. I really think they accepted that fact that things had to change. They knew what the budget was, they were spending the money, and I didn't come in like gangbusters, either. I approached them in a correct way and I think they also respected the fact that I knew a little bit more about cars than Bob did. I was a little bit more towards wanting the project to succeed, perhaps, a little bit more down to earth, nuts and bolts. The fact that I wouldn't be afraid to get my hands dirty doing it. I don't recall that I had any bad experiences...

"Ray Dausman was a problem. But Ray I think, like everybody, had a family. And he looked at the finances and the problem of getting paid, he had to eat, and I think he didn't have any faith, perhaps, that the project was going to be completed and do anything. And I think his job was kinda done, with the engine, and he bailed out a bit after I took over. But he was the only person who bailed, and had any problem with my taking over.

"Part of the problem, like marriage or anything else, was lack of communication, and I don't think Bob was communicating, at least at that level or whatever, and that was a problem too. And I was, I spent more time with it than Bob did because he had a lot of projects going on. Bob had a lot of balls in the air, and you prioritize. I talked a lot with the Reaction Dynamics guys. *The Blue Flame* was low on Bob's priority list because it wasn't quite the chemical engineering challenge that other things were. Once you got IIT guys involved and the mechanical engineering part of it, he was just sorta overseeing that stuff. He wasn't really involved. But he was involved enough to keep that thing going, and as far as I'm concerned he did a great job with all that co-ordination of design, the engine coming together, the wind tunnel tests, all of that."

One of the major factors that delayed the project was the change in the specification of the Goodyear tire specification, from the planned 27-inch diameter to 34.75. That scaled up the size of the car and generated all sorts of knock-on effects.

"Yeah, those kinds of things changed the project. It wasn't so much that the guys at Reaction Dynamics weren't efficient, more that circumstances changed. Looking back at it, we'd have probably been better just run with wheels, no tires at all, which is what people did after that.

"From then on I spent a lot of time and effort that year before we went out to the Flats. We actually took hold of the car and moved it to Chicago, to get Reaction Dynamics' attention, and we had to renegotiate the contract. Initially they were going to end up owning the car, and I'm sorry they didn't."

The loss of the car wasn't the naiveté it might appear on the surface, on Keller and Farnsworth's behalf, as Dietrich explained.

"They had no choice, to be honest with you. In order for the gas industry to put more money into it, they wanted more control. And it was just gonna be that way or we weren't gonna get the project done. It wasn't so much playing hardball as just the way the industry looked at it.

"We did some work on it while it was in Chicago, and got it ready for painting. It had a primer coat and we did some sanding on it."

And then came the infamous ride up to the airport to show it off to a big committee of gas industry heavyweights... *The Blue Flame* crashed while being transported on the Stevenson Expressway.

"It didn't do any damage to the car. Not even the fin. It just went on its side on the trailer, but that didn't hurt the car because it was strapped to the trailer. We kidded about it, because we were gonna do a drop test any how to see if everything would stay together, and we didn't need to do that any longer...

"But that was embarrassing, to say the least. We blocked the Expressway for two hours, and that wasn't very nice. We got a ticket, I think, from the State Police. And we didn't make the meeting of gas industry executives. That was a little embarrassing, too, all these people standing around and we didn't make it... And that was before cell phones, too, so we had to go run and call and do all that sort of stuff... But we got the car back up to Milwaukee and got it on a dragstrip and fired the engine and saw that it ran, and then took it out to the Salt Flats."

Astonishingly, the team got it right almost immediately. The rolling chassis was spot-on from the outset, and the various problems with the engine were to be expected from such experimental engineering. It was an amazing feat to create a car with all that new technology, get it out there and break the record on the first attempt...

"We were, I think, very fortunate to do it in the first year, because we were one of the only American cars that had ever done that." Art Arfons had broken the record in 1964 in his first visit with the *Green Monster*, and Craig Breedlove would later succeed first time out with *Spirit of America - Sonic 1* in 1965, but the latter had encountered all sorts of problems with his first *Spirit of America* back in 1962 and had taken another year to get it sorted out.

"The chassis was wonderful. Gary drove the car down the black line at Bonneville just like he was on the highway. He drove it on the right side of the line going down, and the right side coming back. And it never wavered. I saw pictures of Breedlove when he was driving the *Sonic 1*, and he was all over the track, and lifting the front end. *The Blue Flame* steered beautifully. I would have let my wife drive that thing, I really would have.

"Our problems were getting enough power, having enough fuel. We didn't have big enough fuel capacity because we only had one tank and we coulda used a bigger one. We were getting enough thrust, I believe, but there wasn't enough burn time. When we set the record we went from 90 percent hydrogen peroxide to 98 percent and that extra, plus we had a fairly new catalyst pack that had only done two runs. A lot of people said it was just a peroxide rocket, but we figured the LNG probably gave us at least 100 mph. It was like an afterburner. We couldn't have done it without that. It was somewhat dangerous, the whole operation, mixing the peroxide and the LNG. We had to be careful!

"We had to shove the car at 115 mph before Gary lit the fuse. We were just lucky that Dana Fuller, a cinematographer and former diesel class streamliner record holder, had his van out there that would go that fast. Joe Petrali told me there was no rule against pushing a car. In fact, he told me, laughingly, if we could push at 600 mph that was okay! I told him we were running out of fuel, and we timed it so we would run out in the middle of the mile and coast out.

"There was quite a nice write-up in a newspaper about me afterwards, where it called me the spark that lit *The Blue Flame*. I kind of chuckled about that because somebody's mind picked that up, it wasn't anything I ever said. Out on the Salt Flats, to be honest with you, I think my biggest job was keeping the crew morale up.

Left, Dean Dietrich, IGT business manager, and Gary express relief after finally achieving The Blue Flame's goal; the absolute world land speed record

"I would go round and pound on their doors every morning at six o'clock to get them up and get breakfast and get out there. It was a strenuous six weeks to be out there every day, trying to get the thing going and going right, and keeping the morale up. Because we had bad days and good days."

If anyone ever wanted to do the ultimate team bonding exercise, taking a bunch of guys out to Bonneville and tasking them with running after a speed record is a hell of an effective way to do it. It's a cruel environment, that highlights shortcomings.

"It takes a team, there isn't any individual that isn't indispensable, yet they are all part of the team and everybody has to do their job. And after a while, you keep doing it and it doesn't work, your morale gets down. I also had to keep the gas industry happy and tell them where we were. On top of which we were running out of money, again. And we did run out. We needed to build a new catalyst pack and we needed more hydrogen peroxide, so we needed about $50-60,000, which Henry Linden got for us."

Gary Gabelich once talked of a near mutiny in the team which he had to quell, but Dietrich didn't see it quite that way. "Gary was pretty laidback, he really was, and he didn't participate very much in anything except promoting Gary, to be perfectly honest. And there's nothing wrong with that. And I had no problem with that. He was there to drive the car, he was there to do PR, that's why we hired him, because had a good gab and he was very good with the people that were around. As far as technically and doing anything with the car, Gary sat in the cockpit and drove it. That was fine, because that was his job. He'd tell us anything that he thought was wrong, and that was part of the job too, but he was just the driver. But he was the right guy to do it."

Gabelich was in an interesting position, for he was the first guy in many years who was 'simply' employed to drive the car, rather than the man who had initiated the project in the first place. Parry Thomas, de Hane Segrave, Malcolm and Donald Campbell, George Eyston, John Cobb, Mickey Thompson, Athol Graham, Nathan Ostich, Art Arfons, Craig Breedlove and Richard Noble were all prime movers in their attempts; Glen Leasher, who died at Bonneville in 1962 attempting the record in *Infinity*, and Tom Green who held it for three days with Walt Arfons' *Wingfoot Express* in 1964, were exceptions, though both were part of the groups behind the programs, and Andy Green was chosen by Noble to drive *ThrustSSC*, but prior to that the last 'hired' drivers before Leasher and Tom Green were Englishman Kaye Don in 1930, and Americans Lee Bible and Ray Keech in 1929 and 1928 respectively.

"Gary was a hired gun. He tried to pattern himself after Breedlove and thought he should be getting rich, but we told him: 'Breedlove put that whole project together, he got all the money, and he built the car. Goodyear was his sponsor and they were fighting Firestone. It's totally different with you, Gary. We paid you X dollars to drive this car. You can do what you want with it.' And he didn't unfortunately. They offered him an Indy ride, but they weren't gonna give him thousands of dollars for doing it.

"We paid him $10,000, and on top of which we bought him an insurance policy that cost us almost that much, for his mother. I said to him, 'Gary, I'd rather give you the money than this insurance policy.' But he wanted that. And we let him make anything he wanted after the fact, on public appearances, any of that kind of stuff. And if the gas industry wanted him, he had a rate and he could go and talk. He was free to do any of that. We toured the car for two years, and took it to Europe during that time. Things like the Jochen Rindt Show in Austria. Jochen had just been killed at Monza, but I went over and cut the deal with his widow Nina at her house in Switzerland. She was very lovely, a very nice hostess."

The pressure to succeed at Bonneville was intense; such were the high expectations of the gas industry. "I don't think the gas industry had any realization of how difficult that was, to really do. I think that they'd seen this little *X-1* run and they thought; man, that's a piece of cake. Well, obviously, it wasn't a piece of cake; it's never a piece of cake, any of this stuff. So I felt pressure, but only from inside.

"I had to go back to Chicago for our annual Board of Directors meeting, before we broke the record, and they promoted me to vice-president, which I felt was very good. That didn't depend on this car making it, but I went back out and I felt pretty good about the trust they'd put in me to do all this. So it felt very good to deliver at the time.

"It was one of the few projects, I must say, in all the 30 years working in research and development, that actually met its objectives! I think the original budget was $250,000 and it ended up around $500,000, but it delivered. I don't think that anybody in the gas industry complained. At the time they grumbled, but I think the amount of value publicity-wise was well over that. We had piles of clippings; we had stuff from all over.

"To me, one of the saddest things is that *The Blue Flame* is now in Germany. We toured it for two years and when we got done touring it, it was a case of, 'What are we gonna do with it?' I went to the Smithsonian, and they turned us down. They didn't have room. So then we went down to the Museum of Science and Industry in Chicago, where Breedlove's car sits, and said,

'We got the car that beat Breedlove, kind of a Chicago-based car. Would you guys like to have it?' 'No, we don't have enough room.' So the chairman of the American Gas Association, who had a primary role raising the initial funds with Henry, had a friend in Holland who was a car collector and had approached them, wanting to buy the car. Henry really was in a tough spot because the industry was giving us probably $25,000,000 a year in sponsorship money and so when the guy asks you to do something, you know… Henry came to me and said, 'We are gonna sell the car for what it costs to ship it to Holland. What is that?' It was $10,000 at that time. So that's how it ended up in Holland. At the time I said to Henry, 'I will buy it for $10,000. I'll put it in my back yard and let the neighborhood kids crawl all over it. This is not right.' I don't know what the Sinsheim Museum subsequently paid for it, but it was all a travesty as far as I was concerned. I was just sorry it ever left the U.S..

"If I had to say what my greatest personal achievement was with *The Blue Flame*, I'd say making it work, achieving its goal and keeping the project on the paths you had to do to get there. We did it in the last hour of the last day when it had started raining and before it snowed the next day. I'll tell you, thrashing a crew like that to a successful conclusion was a great achievement for me just as a person, not particularly from my career point of view although it sure didn't hurt it. In Henry Linden's eyes it gave me stature, because the company delivered and I was the fair-haired boy for a little while. But I just felt great personal satisfaction. I look back at it and say it was fun, but it was tough. I think I had the record at the Stateline Café for seven steak dinners in a row because that was the only thing on the menu back then that tasted good!

"And you know, the kind of thing we were doing back then, ecologically, they're talking about doing again now! We've done it already in the gas industry. Fuel cells, liquefied natural gas cars… Yeah, *The Blue Flame* really was Green!"

Pete Farnsworth, Dick Keller, Gary Gabelich, and Dean Dietrich share the triumph

-10-

WENDOVER, A TALE OF TWO CITIES

If you were to Google search "middle of nowhere USA", Wendover, Utah would be prominently listed as a good choice. With apologies to Charles Dickens, this narrative really isn't about Paris and London.

In the late 1960s and early 1970s I had opportunities to experience the western hospitality and rugged ambience of Wendover, Utah. At the time the town was little more than a wide spot on the two-lane US40 road for motorists traveling west to San Francisco. Racing at nearby Bonneville Speedway resulted in my spending a total of about three month's residence in Earl Heath's Western Motel. Having grown up in the "big city" of Chicago, I found the frontier atmosphere of little Wendover to be truly fascinating. In retrospect, I have discovered Wendover to be the most important western town nobody ever heard of.

Driving west out of Salt Lake City at night on my first visit, the black starlit sky hid the landscape as I cruised past Grantsville. Seeing oncoming headlights while motoring along at 70 miles per hour, I dimmed my brights. It would be five minutes before the speeding eastbound car flashed by. Unseen past the headlight beams, the road to Wendover was so perfectly flat and straight that there was no sense of distance at all.

In Wendover free time was spent exploring the nearby hills and desert trails on my motorbike. I found abandoned silver mines bored completely through a mountain and wagon train remains in the muddy desert. At night, shooting jackrabbits on the Nevada dirt roads and losing money playing blackjack at the Stateline Casino, in Nevada, was entertainment. Dinner at the Stateline Café, in Utah, demonstrated the contrasts between the two states it straddled. Along with my meal I would order a chocolate milk shake. When the waitress served me, I asked her to walk over to the bar in the next room, which was in Nevada, and pour a shot of brandy in the shake. She always obliged me and I gave her a nice tip. These are some of my fond memories of that charming town of Wendover.

Wendover City resides on the Utah-Nevada border alongside Interstate Highway I-80. The town is divided between Wendover, Utah and West Wendover, Nevada. While Wendover and West Wendover are really one city straddling two very different states, their populations and economies are totally interdependent. In fact, while Nevada lies in the Pacific Time Zone, West Wendover has opted to run on Utah's Mountain Time Zone. Since the construction of the interstate highway in 1972, with the Mormon dominated Salt Lake City just 120 miles to the east, West Wendover has grown with its gambling resorts, sporting five Casinos. The Utah side, being a morally conservative dry state, has deteriorated with almost no growth since then. The roughly 5,000 person population of West Wendover has grown rapidly from virtually zero since the literal "I-road to prosperity" was completed, while on the east side of the state line, after the Wendover Air Force Base was inactivated in late 1949, the population of 814 has barely doubled in 60 years.

Wendover continues to struggle with almost no business tax base, while West Wendover thrives with the lucrative Nevada gaming and resort industry. Residents of both Wendovers voted to annex the Utah city into Nevada in November, 2002. The citizens believe they are really one (isolated) community and have been divided for too long. Annexation was also endorsed by the states of Nevada and Utah. However, the annexation was permanently halted by the Wendover City Council in 2006. Council members voted it down finally over a financial impasse when Utah would have to pay Nevada $22,000,000 to effect the change. Both Wendovers shared the Junior and Senior High School on the Utah side and the elementary school in Nevada, with the school districts paying each other tuition for the outstate students until 1997. They had also shared police and fire fighting duties. Now there are two separate school districts (Elko County School District serving West Wendover and Tooele School District for Wendover) each having elementary and high schools. The two Wendovers are served by five different police departments; West Wendover Police, Elko County Sheriff, and the Nevada Highway Patrol for West Wendover and Tooele County Sheriff and Utah Highway Patrol on the Utah side. Don't plan on losing pursuing police officers by crossing the border, however, as they will continue in "hot pursuit" without delay.

Wendover relies almost entirely on tourist support businesses like gas stations, motels, stores, and supplies for nearby ranchers while West Wendover has the gambling resort franchise. Wendover also has the nearby potash mining plant as a local employer.

This tiny community that practically nobody ever heard of has played a unique role in the history of the United States. Celebrating their centennial in 2007, Wendoverites proudly noted key local events on a parade float; the 1907 completion of the Western Pacific railroad San Francisco-Salt Lake City line; the 1914 final splice of the transcontinental telephone line; the 1944 formation of the US Army Air Force's 509th Composite Group, training for the first atomic bombardment mission by the *Enola Gay*; and the last American world land speed record at the nearby Bonneville Salt Flats, set by *The Blue Flame* in 1970. Today, those four signal events continue to be celebrated via colorful street banners on Wendover Boulevard.

Wendover centennial celebration features The Blue Flame, Wendover Will, and the transcontinental railroad in 2007

Wendover welcomes major business activity in the late summer every year as land speed racers converge from the four corners of the United States (and the world) for speed events on the nearby Bonneville Salt Flats. Southern California Timing Association (SCTA) Speedweek (3rd week of August); BUB Speed Trials (last week of August); Utah Salt Flats Racing Association (USFRA) World of Speed (2nd week of September); Top Speed Shootout (FIA timed events) follows USFRA; and the SCTA World Finals, in early October, are regularly scheduled organized events featuring hot rods and motorcycles of all sorts. Racers compete in numerous classes, achieving speeds of 200, 300, and some even over 400 miles per hour, where the owners and drivers experience the fruits of their year(s)-long labor, building and tuning exotic (and sometimes not too exotic) speed machines. There can also be a number of private racing sessions for international record setting scheduled around these events. These tourists of speed are appreciated by this tiny community straddling the Utah-Nevada border, since hospitality for travelers is the primary (read only) industry in this gateway to the west.

So, how did a tiny dot on the map become the world's Mecca for speed?

How the West was won!

"Go west, young man!" This paraphrase of Horace Greeley's advice in the August 25, 1838 issue of the *New Yorker* newspaper was heeded by thousands of adventurers and pioneers for the next hundred years. The California Gold Rush, European immigrant influx, and even the Dust Bowls of the early 20th century would cause a steady stream of desperate travelers to pull up their stakes and move hopefully toward the setting sun.

In July of 1847 Mormon pioneers began entering the Salt Lake Valley, emigrating en masse after years of persecution in the Midwest. When Brigham Young declared "This is the right place. Drive on!" their search for a home was over. Salt Lake City was born. However, for other adventurous Americans the vast westward migration had just begun.

From 1846 until 1848, the United States was at war with Mexico. Finally victorious, President James K. Polk, a believer in the Manifest Destiny of the U.S., concluded the conflict by signing the Treaty of Guadalupe Hidalgo on February 2. Second in importance only to the purchase of Manhattan Island by Peter Minuit for an assortment of hardware, the United States acquired 525,000 square miles of land for $15,000,000. This acquisition included California, Texas, major portions of Arizona and New Mexico, western Colorado, Nevada, Utah, and part of Wyoming.

Almost coincidentally, on January 24, a gold nugget was discovered at John Sutter's sawmill in Coloma, California, just northeast of Sacramento. Polk, eager to reap political advantage for his foresight, later addressed the U.S. Congress on December 5, 1848 stating, "It was known that mines of the precious metals existed to a considerable extent in California at the time of its acquisition. Recent discoveries render it probable that these mines are more extensive and valuable than was anticipated. The accounts of the abundance of gold in that territory are of such extraordinary character as would scarcely command belief."

With that speech, the California Gold Rush was joined. From 1848 through 1855 some 300,000 adventurers flooded into the state. Easterners, including many new immigrants looking for their fortunes, could avoid making the arduous and dangerous cross country journey sailing by ship through the Drake Passage around Cape Horn. Midwestern gold seekers, however, prepared for an overland journey. Wagon trains formed on the eastern shore of the Missouri River at the steamboat ports of St. Joseph, Independence, and Council Bluffs to be led westward by experienced guides. The next 2,000 miles of their trek would prove trying and hazardous. Averaging 10 to 15 miles per day, water, feed for the animals, and provisions required careful planning and some luck to complete the journey safely.

Heading west across the Great American Desert, first on the old Oregon Trail established in the early 19th century by fur traders, the early California-bound pioneers and their "prairie schooners" veered southwest from Fort Hall in Idaho to join the California Trail beginning around 1843. Most of the trip was actually on foot since the hard ride of the unsprung covered wagons could be tiring and painful. Reliable guides and seasonal timing were crucial to a successful journey. Wagon trains would necessarily follow rivers and hunt game en route for sustenance. Draft animals could graze in the vast western plains along the trails. Spring rains would imperil the early travelers with their wagons bogging down on the dirt trails. Late summer travelers would often find the trails over-grazed, endangering their animals and their own survival as well.

This first edition of the California Trail, staying north of the Great Salt Lake, was bedeviled by rough country that made the trip quite arduous. Alternative routes were continually sought by the mercenary guides. It was tempting to cross south of the lake through Salt Lake City and then west to Nevada and across the Great Basin to California, avoiding much of the mountainous terrain.

The Great Salt Lake Desert beckons.

Frontiersman explorer Jedediah Smith had previously made the first recorded crossing of the Great Salt Lake Desert, traveling east from California in 1827. Having on earlier journeys survived three Indian massacres and a grizzly bear attack which literally scalped him, the Great Basin stretching from Reno to Salt Lake City nearly did him in. His party needed to get 1,500 pounds of beaver pelts to a planned rendezvous in the Cache Valley at Bear Lake, northeast of the Great Salt Lake. "Diah's" journal recounts the treacherous journey across the Nevada desert and around the southern shore of the lake, from June 23rd through July 3rd. Surviving starvation, continuous thirst, loss of animals and nearly loss of their lives, the emaciated party finally arrived at their destination camp. A few years after this ordeal Jedediah was murdered by Comanches while looking for water on the Santa Fe Trail.

Tales of Smith's ordeal did not tempt many professional guides to try the southern route. In 1841, however, the shorter route west would again seem compelling. On May 15, a wagon train made up of some 70 pioneers gathered near Independence, Missouri. With the inexperienced "Captain" John Bartleson leading, 2 carts and 15 wagons set out for California. John Bidwell, one of the emigrants in the party, kept copious notes of their historic journey, which historians have later named the Bartleson-Bidwell Party.

Initially, the group headed west on the Oregon Trail joining forces with a party of Catholics led by a renowned mountain man, Thomas "Broken Hand" Fitzpatrick. Upon reaching Fort Hall, Idaho, the Bartleson party turned south, while about half this original group continued west on the proven Oregon Trail. Now down to 32 people and 9 wagons, they planned to traverse the north shore of the Great Salt Lake and then drive southwest across the barren salt desert to Nevada. Bartleson and two companions rode ahead to seek trail directions while the slower wagon train traveled on a southwest bearing, intending to rejoin them at Cache Valley. Headed towards the Bear River in mid-August, they became the first wagon train to enter northern Utah. At that point the party became lost for several weeks and eventually looped back since there was no experienced guide.

Bartleson noted in his journal at this point, "This is the fruit of having no pilot – we pass through cash valley (sic), where we intended to stop and did not know it." Late in August Bartleson finally caught up with the group. They rumbled on through Park Valley, Bidwell noting that food was scarce, no fresh water was to be found for man nor beast, and grazing unavailable. Traveling about 10 miles per day, in a week they finally arrived at Pilot Peak where they could re-provision with a watering hole and abundant vegetation. There was still more hardship to endure in the Great Basin, eventually losing all their wagons and trekking on foot for five months over the Sierra Nevada mountains, finally arriving at John Sutter's ranch in northern California in November.

Coincidentally, Bidwell worked for Sutter for many years and when gold was later discovered at Sutter's Fort in 1848, he personally delivered the news to San Francisco, thereby initiating the California Gold Rush.

Even before then the pace of immigration west had continued to grow with the promise of fertile lands and forests beyond the Sierra Nevada and Cascade mountains. At this time the United States government also began looking to The West for further expansion under the popular notion of Manifest Destiny. The U.S War Department commissioned John Charles Fremont to explore regions west of the Rocky Mountains. As a captain in the U.S. Topographical Corps, Fremont led five well-documented expeditions exploring and mapping the unknown region between the Rocky Mountains and the Pacific and was nicknamed "Pathfinder". He enlisted the experienced frontiersman Christopher "Kit" Carson as a guide through these rugged Indian territories. Carson's many years spent living among the Indian tribes made him a welcome figure there, and he spoke their language as well as his own.

Three of Captain Fremont's expeditions took him through Utah. In the spring of 1845, General Winfield Scott sent him on his third expedition to explore the Great Basin (which comprises western Utah, all of Nevada, and California east of the Sierra Nevadas) and onward to the maritime region of California and

Oregon. This trip was of great importance because he was able to finally determine that the Great Basin was an enclosed interior bowl and forever end the myth of a water passage, the Rio Buenaventura erroneously mapped in 1778 by Barnardo de Miera, to the Pacific coast. The War Department saw value in finding a shorter route to the Pacific coast, anticipating the need for rapid troop movements in the upcoming Mexican-American War (1846-1848). Traversing a southern route around the Great Salt Lake, Fremont's party entered Utah via the White River and Uinta Basin, followed the Provo River to Utah Lake and then up to the southern shore of the Great Salt Lake.

After two weeks of exploring the lake and Antelope Island, Fremont pulled up stakes and headed west again. Reaching the summit of Cedar Mountain in a few days, the vast white expanse of the Great Salt Lake Desert lay before him. In the distance, beyond the salt plain, he could see another high mountain peak over sixty miles away which would later be named Pilot Peak. That prominent landmark could guide his expedition across the featureless desert. Crossing the desert with his whole party, not knowing if water was there, would be too risky. So Fremont dispatched Kit Carson and three of his men on the best horses, and with extra supplies, to reconnoiter.

The next day Carson found the spring (now called Donner Spring) at the base of Pilot Peak and lit a signal fire to alert Fremont it was safe to cross. Fremont's party was then able to negotiate this barren salt desert of the Great Basin confident of replenishing their water and grazing for the horses. This lonely oasis would become the raison d'être for the eventual City of Wendover. Strategically located midway between Salt Lake City and the Humboldt River, it made a safe haven for the adventurous travelers yet to come. After finally arriving in California at Sutter's Fort, Fremont sent a letter describing the new route which was published in several eastern newspapers. This discovery renewed interest in pioneers to migrate west.

Hastings Cutoff

Lansford Hastings encountered Fremont at Sutter's Fort and they discussed his shortcut in detail. Hastings quickly published a guide, *"The Emigrant's Guide to Oregon and California"*, describing the cutoff. Then, seeing an opportunity to profit from this discovery, in April, 1846 he set up camp near the Sweetwater River in Wyoming and sent a man east with a letter inviting eager emigrants traveling the California Trail to join him at Fort Bridger from where he would lead them across the Hastings Cutoff.

Tragically, as it later turned out, on April 16, 1846 James Fraser Reed departed from Springfield, Illinois leading a group of covered wagons destined for Sutter's Fort in California. He planned to follow the route described in Hastings' guide book which promised to save the pioneers 350 to 400 miles on their westward trek. Coincidentally, on that very day, Lansford Hastings began his journey east from California to see what his advertised shortcut was really like.

Joined by other wagons in Fort Laramie, a letter arrived from Hastings stating he would meet the Reed group at Fort Bridger and guide them south of the Great Salt Lake on his cutoff. Upon reaching the Little Sandy River in Wyoming the trail split into two routes, Hastings' untested cutoff and the well-traveled northern trail. Here the caravan divided, with the majority staying north of the Great Salt Lake and the rest, with George Donner newly elected captain, heading south. Donner's group finally numbered 87 pioneers in 23 wagons.

Traversing the Wasatch Mountains, progress was severely retarded, only managing to cover less than two miles per day. On August 30 they began crossing the Great Salt Lake Desert, planning to make it in two days. Wagons and equipment would have to be abandoned as they became mired in the deep wet salty mud. Five days later with their water supply nearly exhausted they reached the spring at the base of Pilot Peak.

Edwin Bryan recorded in his diary upon finding the first signs of water, "Men and mules on their first arrival, as we learned, had madly rushed into the stream and drank together of its muddy waters… we would trace the small stream of water until we could find the fountain spring. After considerable search among the reeds, willow, and luxuriant grass, we discovered a spring. …the next morning the basin was sounded to thirty-five feet, and no bottom found."

During a later expedition to survey the Great Salt Lake area, Captain Howard Stansbury of the U.S. Topographical Corps wrote of his coming upon what is now called Donner Springs: "…we came to the southern point of the mountain, where there had been an encampment of emigrants… there were several large springs of excellent water and the encampment had apparently been quite a large one. Clothes, books, cases of medicine, wagon wheels, tools, &c., lay strewn about, abandoned by their owners, who had brought them two thousand miles only to throw them away."

Continuing on their westward travel, the unfortunate Donner party met continuous delaying challenges until they became stranded in the Sierra Nevada Mountains with early winter snows. Already depleted of food supplies they suffered grave hardship and starvation over several months. Ultimately, resulting to cannibalism, only forty-six of the ill-fated eighty-seven survived. While two-thirds of the men had perished, two-thirds of the women and children lived to be rescued.

Though hazardous, this route still remained popular through the early years of the California Gold Rush in 1849 and 1850. Later, in 1850, Hensley's Salt Lake Cutoff developed a new route around the northern end of the Great Salt Lake which completely avoided the harrowing, desolate salt desert stretch. The end of the Mormon Trail east of Salt Lake City eventually became the terminus of the short-lived Hastings Cutoff. Pilot Peak and its nearby Donner Spring became redundant and isolated once more.

The Iron Horse arrives.

Railroad transportation would soon displace the hazardous stagecoach lines and slower wagon trains that continued to populate The West. Following the end of the Civil War, work began on the first transcontinental railroad, the Overland Route. The Central Pacific Railroad of California began laying track from the west while the Union Pacific railroad commenced building from the east, starting from Omaha, Nebraska at the Missouri River. The "Last Spike" was driven at Promontory Summit, Utah on May 10, 1869. These trains shortened the trip to 8 days (from several months) in the comfort of a carriage seat, but their route went north of the Great Salt Lake to Oakland, California. It was still necessary to ferry the trains across the Missouri River to connect with the existing eastern rail network. However, both Denver and Salt Lake City, the two largest cities in the Great American Desert were not being served.

Finally, in 1903 the Western Pacific Railroad was organized in California, financed by George Jay Gould. This would eventually become one of the west's most popular railroads connecting Salt Lake City to Oakland, California. On January 2, 1906 Western Pacific began laying track heading east from Oakland, followed on May 24 when they began building west from Salt Lake City. In May, 1907, Western Pacific track was completed from Salt Lake City to the Nevada state line where Wendover became the division point on Western Pacific's Eighth Subdivison. The rails were laid upon a 50-mile-long causeway laid on the salt pan, comprised of rock and gravel, at a great cost. It would be more than two years, December 1, 1909, before freight service would actually begin between Salt Lake City and Oakland.

Water has always been the reason for Wendover's existence. With the coming of the railroad, the steam engines now required frequent liquid refreshment. The company built a water tower at Wendover, piping the fluid twenty-three miles from Pilot Springs. Wendover had a small train depot and was a crew change point where the trains would also take on water and coal. Allegedly, the city's name was borrowed from the Western Pacific's surveyor, Charles Wendover, who laid out the company town plat.

Wendover's railroad facilities included a double ended siding more than a mile long to allow trains traveling in opposite directions on the single track to pass by. There also was a five-track yard for assembling trains, with a roundhouse and a wye that allowed a locomotive to reverse direction, providing a turning point for the locomotives.

Of note, the 43.7 miles of track between Wendover (mile post 806.3) and mile post 850, about midway between Knolls and Clive, is the longest straight and level railroad track in the United States. Following World War II, diesel locomotives began replacing the high maintenance steam behemoths. Finally, in June 1972, the crew change point in Wendover was eliminated as crews operated the full distance between Salt Lake City and Elko, Nevada. The Eighth Subdivision of the railroad was eliminated at that time.

Mr. Watson, come here...

AT&T had begun building the country's original long-distance telephone network in 1885. The network reached from New York City to Chicago by 1892. As a telephone signal travels along the copper wire conductor it weakens. So, that distance was the longest practical for a thick copper wire. Loading coils were developed in 1899 and allowed the signal to travel a little farther; the network reaching Denver, Colorado by 1911. Again, the practical signal transmission limit had been reached.

AT&T's President Theodore Vail had made the transcontinental telephone line a company priority in 1908, knowing the technology was not yet in existence. Chief Engineer John J. Caty made a commitment the following year in San Francisco when he claimed the company would have a transcontinental line operational in time for the city's planned 1915 Panama-Pacific Exposition.

Caty hired scientists to study the problem of amplifying the electrical signals which would be necessary to meet his challenge. AT&T announced to the scientific and engineering community that the company would reward an inventor of an amplifying device. Dr. Lee DeForest presented his prototype which he called the "audion", a three-element vacuum tube, in October, 1912. The audion fizzled quickly in his first demonstration to the AT&T scientists, but the problem was quickly resolved. By the following summer, having acquired DeForest's patent, AT&T had tested high-vacuum tube amplifiers on a long-distance network. That fall they began stringing the line west from Denver and upgrading the line back to the east with amplifiers.

Finally, on June 17, 1914, the transcontinental telephone line's last pole was erected in (you guessed it) Wendover, Utah and the final connection made. Conveniently, the telephone line paralleled the Western Pacific Railroad's tracks which also transported the poles and copper wire spools for building the line.

Transcontinental telephone lines are prominent in historic downtown Wendover photo

Not wanting to waste the opportunity for publicity at the opening of the San Francisco Exposition, the first transcontinental telephone conversation was linked on January 25, 1915. This was a four-way hookup connecting the cities of New York (Alexander Graham Bell), San Francisco (Thomas

Watson, Bell's assistant on the very first telephone call), Jekyll Island, Georgia (Theodore Vail), and Washington, D.C. (President Woodrow Wilson at the White House). Asked to repeat the very first words he had spoken on the original telephone call, Edison said, "Mr. Watson, come here, I want you." Watson, with a grin on his face replied, "It would take me a week now."

Age of the Automobile

At the dawn of the twentieth century, Americans began their love affair with the automobile. The old rutted country roads, which were barely adequate for horse drawn wagons, now needed to be paved to accommodate the higher speeds of horseless carriages. The newly mechanized US Army also had a strategic need for a transcontinental highway.

Named to honor fallen heroes of the Great War, a route for the Victory Highway was laid out from New York City to San Francisco roughly along the fortieth parallel in 1921. The Wendover Cutoff was designated as part of that highway and received federal funding under the Federal Highways Act of 1921 for completion. A 24-foot-wide causeway was built parallel and just north of the Western Pacific Railroad's tracks using clay fill. The final road surface was a layer of gravel hauled in by the Western Pacific from its gravel pits west of Wendover. This section was finally completed in 1924. In 1926, the federal government instituted a road numbering system, replacing the old named highway designations, and the Victory Highway became known as United States Route 40 (US40) passing right through Wendover. This popular two-lane cross-country highway was eventually upgraded in 1969 to Interstate 80, which now skirts the city to the north.

William "Bill" Smith arrived in town when he was unceremoniously thrown off the Western Pacific train as it briefly stopped at the Wendover depot in 1924. Bill was an unemployed mechanic heading east from San Francisco looking for opportunity, but didn't have a ticket. Having an entrepreneur's optimism, though, he saw opportunity in the remoteness of this outpost on the newly designated US40 highway. Partnered with Herman Eckstein, Bill opened the cobblestone State Line Service station where travelers could refuel both their cars and stomachs as well, located as named right on the Utah-Nevada state line. They erected a tall pole alongside the building with a bright electric light that burned around the clock. Driving west on US40 from Salt Lake City, drivers could see the beacon from over forty miles away. This attracted customers like moths to a flame. When Herman passed away, Bill and Herman's son decided there wasn't sufficient income for both of them and tossed a coin, winner takes all. Bill won.

Nevada's state legislature legalized gambling in 1931 and another light bulb went on in Bill's brain. He had just purchased the State Line Hotel and commenced installing a roulette table to entertain the guests. In 1935 the state of Nevada licensed the new State Line Hotel & Casino which would become the longest continually licensed gambling establishment in the state until it was sold in January of 2003.

The Mormon Meteor shines the motor sports spotlight on Bonneville

David Abbott "Ab" Jenkins was born in Spanish Fork, Utah in 1883 and his parents moved to Salt Lake City in 1887. Because Salt Lake City was a hotbed of bicycle and motorcycle racing at the turn of the twentieth century, it was known as "the

178

birthplace of speed". Young Jenkins, being adventurous was bitten by the motorbike bug, competing on dirt tracks and cross-country races. He eventually had a successful business career in the Salt Lake community as a building contractor.

As he outgrew that youthful fascination with motorcycles Ab purchased an automobile in 1906. As a family man, he eschewed participating in dangerous massed start track racing and developed a passion for driving endurance events. Jenkins set two cross-country records in an automobile but finally stopped point-to-point record runs out of concern for safety on open roads with increasing traffic.

When the Wendover Cutoff portion of the Victory Highway was completed in 1924, one of the highway's builders, who knew his reputation, asked Ab to race the train from Salt Lake City to Wendover as part of the road's inaugural celebration. Jenkins agreed, and beat the train by five minutes. In 1926 he set the cross-country record from New York City to San Francisco in 86 hours and 20 minutes. Then, in 1928 he raced on a board track for 24 hours setting records again. Being familiar with the Bonneville Salt Flats near Wendover, Ab then began his record-breaking career on the flat, hard as concrete, natural speedway.

Land speed racing originally began on paved highways in Europe. As speeds reached 80 miles per hour, then soared to over 100 miles per hour, other venues were sought for safety and smooth, flat surfaces. Henry Ford drove his *999* racer on frozen Lake St. Clair in 1904 at 91 miles per hour. Then, Daytona Beach in Florida and Pendine Sands in England saw increasing speeds, up to 174 miles per hour in England. Malcolm Campbell in *Blue Bird II* set the last world land speed record in Europe in February, 1927. The following month, Henry Segrave drove his 1,000 horsepower Sunbeam to 202 miles per hour at Daytona

Beach and the USA became the playground for these merchants of speed. Finally, the last world land speed record to be set on the beach was 276 miles per hour by Malcolm Campbell in March, 1935.

Ab Jenkins concentrated on setting closed course endurance records on the Bonneville Salt Flats. He had done some consulting for the Pierce-Arrow automobile company, helping design a new 12-cylinder engine producing almost 200 horsepower. In 1932 he convinced Pierce-Arrow that he would set a 24-hour endurance record demonstrating the speed and reliability of their new powerplant. Claiming he would be able to drive over 2,400 miles in 24 hours, they agreed to lend him the car. A 10 mile circular course was laid out on the salt and the timers and crew worked in shifts as he manhandled the mechanical beast solo for 24 hours. Refueling every two hours, Ab never left his seat for the whole 24 hours drive. Jenkins averaged almost 113 miles per hour and drove the Pierce-Arrow 2,710 miles that day, September 18 and 19. Timed with stopwatches and having no official timers present, American Automobile Association (AAA) did not certify this attempt. More attempts would follow.

Returning the next year with the same car and official AAA sanction, Ab set his first official records. Early on a storm blew over the salt flats, but Ab kept motoring. Even Mother Nature could not slow him down on that day. After his last gas stop, and nearing 24 hours at a grueling pace, he pulled out a razor and shaved to look presentable at the finish. This time he had the record at 117 miles per hour. Returning, again, in 1934 the trusty Pierce-Arrow notched still another record at 127 miles per hour.

Jenkins had newsreel films of this last effort, so he took them to Daytona in March 1935 to convince Campbell to bring his *Blue Bird* to run on the Bonneville Salt Flats. Following this exhortation Campbell, John Cobb, and George Eyston came west to have a go on the salt. That summer Wendover and the Bonneville Salt Flats became christened as the Mecca of land speed racing.

Actually, the first land speed record attempt at Bonneville had occurred 21 years earlier. "Wild Bob" Burman had set an AAA sanctioned world land speed record of 141.37 miles per hour on the Florida beaches at Daytona on April 23, 1911, driving the monstrous 1300 cubic inch, 200 horsepower *Blitzen Benz*. After race car engine sizes were later restricted by AAA, the now obsolete race car was purchased by race promoter Ernie Moross who had a barnstorming team of fast racing cars. "Terrible" Teddy Tetzlaff, who had competed in four Indianapolis 500 mile races, was now driving Moross' Benz. Moross promoted a railroad excursion on the Western Pacific from Salt Lake City to Wendover, there being no passable road at that time. The mighty Benz was unloaded from the train on August 11, 1914 and then raced across the salt with a mighty roar from the unmuffled engine allegedly heard all the way into town. While stopwatches reportedly caught Tetzlaff's time in the mile at 25.4 seconds, for 141.73 miles per hour, there was no AAA sanction for the event and so the time remains "unofficial". But the event did signal to the world that a great new land speed record venue was awaiting there in Utah.

In July of 1935, after Jenkins had once again set stock car world records for endurance up to 24 hours, John Cobb arrived at Bonneville to up the ante in his *Napier-Railton Special*. Cobb's record of 134.85 mph handily eclipsed Ab's previous 24-hour best of 127.229 mph set the year earlier. Although his records were broken, he was enthused to see his beloved salt flats becoming the ultimate speed venue.

Now the world land speed records would begin to fall. Malcolm Campbell had set the mile record at 276.16 mph on Daytona Beach sand in March of that year. However, he knew there was more speed in his giant Campbell-Railton *Bluebird* speedster. Imperfections in the natural beach surface were causing his wheels to lose traction. Following Cobb and Captain Eyston to Bonneville, Campbell set the first official world land speed record on the salt flats, and the first over 300 mph (301.129) on September 3, 1935. From this point forward, until 1970, all world land speed records would be set on this remote salt desert just east of Wendover.

Wendover goes to war – and wins!

In Europe, World War II began in September, 1939. The United States was committed at that time to remaining neutral but began contingency planning for war. Congress approved funds in 1940 for acquiring land to be used for bomber training and gunnery ranges. Because of the vast uninhabited desert terrain in western Utah, it was considered an ideal site. Ultimately, nearly two million acres were incorporated into the Utah Test and Training Range, the world's largest military reserve in land area.

Wendover Air Field was located just south of the town center. Although its remoteness would be an asset for security purposes, the nearby Western Pacific railroad was a strategic asset as well, connecting the base with both coasts. Construction on the air base began on September 20, 1940. Water, still being scarce in the desert, was piped some 32 miles from Johnson's Springs to meet the increasing demand of the military population. Wendover, at the time, was still primarily a railroad town with a population of only 272 citizens. By late 1943 there were some 2,000 civilian and 17,500 military personnel stationed at Wendover. For much of the war Wendover Air Field and surrounding area was the Army Air Force's only bombing and gunnery range.

The secret Wendover Air Base was the training site for the atomic bombers in World War II

America was plunged into the war on December 7, 1941 with the Japanese Pearl Harbor attack and Hitler declaring war on the United States. On April 26th, 1942 the first of the training groups arrived in Wendover, consisting of the 306th Bomb Group flying B-17s. They would become the first Army Air Force unit to daylight bomb Germany flying out of England. In all, some 21 heavy bomb groups would train in Wendover during the war. Eventually, by the end of the war, the base contained 668 buildings including 361 housing units for married officers and civilians. This was a big change from 1942, when

Bob Hope's USO troupe visited to entertain the airmen and he called the place "Leftover Field".

The most significant mission initiated at Wendover Air Field was the one that ended World War II, Operation Silverplate. At the urging of a group of American scientists, Albert Einstein prominent among them, President Roosevelt authorized the top secret "Manhattan Project" to design and build the atomic bomb the day before Japan's unprovoked Pearl Harbor attack. Development of the atomic weapon moved at a brisk pace and in late 1943 General Groves, commander of the Manhattan Project, ordered the Army Air Force to commence preparing to drop the bombs on Germany and Japan. Project Alberta was initiated to fulfill the crucial mission.

Project Alberta was carried out in a remote area of the Wendover Air Field complex. It consisted of three elements; design the bomb shape and build it, ballistic testing of the atomic bomb design (Project W-47) and modification of B-29s to deliver it (Project Silverplate), and training the crews in preparation for deployment overseas.

Operation Silverplate was the project to convert B-29s to carry the atom bombs, here loading the dummy Fat Man bomb for bombing practice

General "Hap" Arnold selected Colonel Paul W. Tibbetts, Jr. to form and train a bomb group singularly tasked with dropping the atomic bomb. The new 509th Composite Group was formed at Wendover Field to execute Silverplate. Ultimately over 800 personnel were transferred into this group for training. Project W-47 supplied the unit with prototype atomic bombs (without the explosives) for evaluation of the designs and bomber crew training. These dummy bombs (called "pumpkins") were loaded into the modified B-29s and then dropped over Wendover's bombing range. The pilots were instructed to perform a sharp turn maneuver immediately upon release of the bomb in order to mitigate the blast effect on the plane. Two completely different atomic fission bomb designs were eventually evolved, the Fat Man and the Little Boy. Between October, 1944 and August, 1945 155 test missions were flown, the Fat Man being dropped at the Salton Sea Naval Air Station Range and the Little Boy at Wendover. Finally, on

The Little Boy dummy is lowered into the loading pit where it will be hoisted into the B-29 for bombing practice

August 4, a Fat Man containing high explosives was dropped at Wendover, completing Project W-47.

The 509th Composite Group arrived at Tinian Island in late spring and immediately began flying combat missions, dropping more pumpkins. On August 6, 1945 Colonel Tibbetts flew his B-29, Enola Gay, and dropped the Little Boy on Hiroshima, Japan. Three days later Major Charles Sweeney flew another B-29, Bock's Car, dropping the Fat Man on Nagasaki. A second Fat Man was loaded onto another B-29 at Wendover on August 14, ordered by Colonel Tibbetts when the Japanese didn't immediately surrender. However, the order was countermanded while the plan was just off the California coast after the Japanese finally responded. This ended World War II.

Hotrodders invade Wendover

Almost coincident with the mass production of automobiles in the early 20th century arose the "need for speed". Owners of mundane family vehicles sought speed tips and simple modifications to increase their performance. Early measures of superiority were hill climbs, acceleration duels, and top speed. In the Los Angeles area in the 1920s good roads, good weather, and youthful exuberance resulted in impromptu street racing becoming a nuisance. As the population grew, law enforcement put pressure on these outlaw "hotrodders" to take their speed business elsewhere.

The Mojave Desert beckoned. Rosamond, El Mirage, Harper, Muroc and other dry lakes became speed laboratories for testing their modified street machines. Being close to Los Angeles, eventually large crowds would gather to race cars and watch the action. It became important to know how fast the cars would go and whose were fastest. Improvised timing lanes were marked out and speeds measured with stop watches. All of this high speed recreation was dangerous, both for drivers and onlookers. It became apparent there needed to be some organization before a disaster would end the fun. Local hot rod clubs banded together to form grass-roots organizations; Russetta Timing Association, Bell Timing Association, and Mojave Timing Association to address safety concerns and more accurate speed measurements.

Land speed racing began, and has remained, largely an amateur do-it-yourself sporting activity. That's how it began, and that's how it remains, with some exceptions. Volunteers from local car clubs helped set up the courses, inspected the racing vehicles, provided crowd security, and helped the timers at these race meetings. Eventually, the racing enthusiasts settled on Muroc Dry Lake as the most convenient and safest venue. In late 1937, seven of these active car clubs formed the Southern California Timing Association. Two founding clubs, the Road Runners and the Sidewinders continue to be active in the SCTA today. They began SCTA-organized racing at Muroc in 1938.

The Army Air Corps had built nearby Muroc Field as a base to service aircraft using the Rodgers Dry Lake bombing range in the early 1930s. As World War II began in Europe, the base was expanded for experimental aircraft flight testing. The Army annexed Muroc Dry Lake, taking advantage of the flat terrain described by General "Hap" Arnold as "level as a billiard table." Eventually, the back-up runway for the Space Shuttle landings would follow the same route that saw hotrodders racing in the pre-war days.

Following the war, SCTA moved land speed racing to El Mirage Dry Lake. El Mirage continues to be used for land speed racing to this day. SCTA schedules 6 race weekends, but the speeds are necessarily slower than would have been possible on the longer old Muroc course.

When John Cobb returned to post-war Bonneville in 1947 with his Railton streamliner to raise the world land speed record to almost 400 miles per hour, it caught the attention of the SCTA hotrodders. SCTA Road Runners club members Wally Parks and "Pete" Petersen arranged a series of meetings in 1948 and 1949 with "Gus" Bachman of the Utah Chamber of Commerce in Salt Lake City to present their plans for racing hot rods on the Bonneville Salt Flats. Bachman, whose job was to promote Utah businesses, thought this type of event could help the economy of little Wendover. Utah had already designated the salt desert as an "Automobile Testing Area", so it wasn't too difficult convincing his superiors of this idea.

Amazed at their success, the SCTA delegation came back to Los Angeles with a one year contract to use the course. Then they had to convince the larger SCTA membership to use their treasury supporting this more distant racing venue. Thirty six competitors arrived in Wendover that first year. Dean Batchelor drove the *So-Cal Special* streamliner to a one way speed of 193.54 miles per hour in August 1949. The following year two cars actually exceeded 200 miles per hour. And, so, the hot rod invasion began.

Now every summer and fall hundreds of eager land speed racers and thousands of spectators and supporters converge on Wendover for their "speed fix". There are no prizes of any material value – merely recognition from their fellow competitors that they are the fastest or most innovative in their class. That is truly priceless.

-11-
CAPTAIN BONNEVILLE – THIS IS THE PLACE

The famous Bonneville Salt Flats is part of ancient Lake Bonneville, which now comprises 4000 square miles of the Great Salt Lake Desert. Formed 30,000 years ago, in the Pleistocene Epoch, a 46 square mile area of hard salt pan is now used for high-speed automobile and motorcycle record attempts.

A sign on Interstate-80 announces the Bonneville Salt Flats to passersby

The area is named for Captain Benjamin Louis Eulalie de Bonneville, a Paris-born U.S. graduate of the US Military Academy, who ran a fur trading company in the Rocky Mountains while on furlough in the 1830s. In 1833, trapper and legendary frontiersman Joseph R. Walker mapped and explored the area around the Great Salt Lake while working for the company run by Captain Bonneville. In those days, it was common for fur trappers to name significant landmarks after their employers, perhaps in an effort to gain favor or better wages. It is from Walker's maps that the salt flats and ancient lake derive their name, although there is no historical record to show that Bonneville himself ever saw the area that bears his name.

After a good night's sleep at the Western Motel in Utah's western border town of Wendover, 15 miles from the Salt Flats, on Tuesday, September 15, the crew prepared the gleaming pearlescent blue and white car for running under a clear blue sky and in warm sunshine. Wheel bearings and races had to be changed as a precaution after transporting the car over 1,500 miles. Parachutes were packed for the first time by Jim Deist, the Glendale-based pioneer of the drogue braking system that was used by so many high-speed dragsters, and all the last-minute details were carefully completed and checked off. Finally, in the laborious process known as 'de-fodding', Gary and the crew walked the entire 13-mile length of the International Course and run-off areas picking up debris that might cause problems for the tires on the high-speed runs.

On Thursday, September 17, we assembled the crew and Gary before dawn for an early morning photo session. Keeping in mind the arbitrary nature of the weather at Bonneville, I was anxious to get the show on the road as quickly as possible. After all the photographers were appeased, *The Blue Flame* was rolled down to the south end of the measured mile to begin a series of acceleration tests. After loading a small quantity of hydrogen peroxide and LNG on board, Gary was strapped into the padded cockpit. In a nice touch, this had been upholstered by the late Chuck Suba's father. Gary hooked up his breathing system and radio, the canopy was fastened down and the first countdown began. "5, 4, 3, 2, 1 ..." BANG! An orange ball of flame shot from the tailpipe and the car accelerated out of sight on a four-second burst of power. Our baby was at last running under its own power for the first time!

Inspecting the car afterward, the source of the unexpected noise was traced to a small explosion in the first-stage LNG injectors. The intricate weldment may have been stress-cracked during the earlier static testing at Great Lakes Dragaway. I had asked Gary to roll into the throttle to prevent a 'wet start' from the cold hydrogen peroxide catalyst, which was also maybe part of the problem. Anyway, an explosive mixture of oxygen from the decomposed hydrogen peroxide and gaseous methane (natural gas) violently ruptured the LNG heat exchanger section of the fuel injectors. This was a serious setback, but although the damaged injectors could not be used it was decided to continue running with just hydrogen peroxide, at reduced thrust, to observe the handling characteristics of the car at speed. This also gave me some time to work out a plan to repair the rocket motor.

Over the next few days the speed was increased to a maximum of 429 mph, but then it began falling off. Noting that the damaged injectors were deforming and restricting the exhaust flow, we pulled the engine on September 22 to effect repairs. I drove into Salt Lake City with Gerard and proceeded to redesign and reconfigure the LNG injectors and catalyst pack at Mountain Fuel Supply's maintenance shop. Mountain was a sponsor of the project through AGA, and was very supportive throughout. The first-stage LNG heat exchanger/injectors could not be replaced in a reasonable period of time so the entire first-stage injector was discarded and the second-stage injector array moved forward in the combustion chamber. Running the engine again would be the only way to determine if the catalyst pack screens were damaged. Being pure silver wire mesh, the melting point was just above normal operating temperature. If the screens were degraded they would begin to melt farther and block the propellant flow as we continued to run the rocket.

Back in Wendover, at Earl Heath's famous Western Service station, Pete was repairing hairline cracks which had appeared in the inner walls of the rocket chamber. We reassembled the motor and the *Flame* was ready to run on the 25th.

What a run it was! Gary took off like a jackrabbit and laid down a 300 plus mph smokescreen two miles long. This sight would become a popular dramatic photo of *The Blue Flame*.

Pete and I knew instantly the rocket combustion chamber catalyst screens were shot. The melting point of the silver catalyst screens is 1763 °F and the rocket motor's downstream combustion chamber temperature with the LNG was over 2500°F. With the backflow of the flame front from the earlier ruptured injector weldment, the screens at the rear of the catalyst had melted, were restricting the hydrogen peroxide decomposition reaction, and blowing raw hydrogen peroxide out the nozzle. The entire crew felt the huge disappointment after having toiled around the clock for two days readying the car. But this was only a taste of what was to come.

This time, we towed *The Blue Flame* to a little-used retired Air Force base just outside Wendover. The remote site was where the WWII atomic bomber crews (509th Composite Group – B29s) had trained for their missions over Japan. While Pete and our crew dismantled the engine once again, I was calling all over the country to line up materials necessary for assembling a new catalyst pack. The essential pure silver wire screen could not be available for six to eight weeks. Given the urgency of beating the coming winter storms, this was not acceptable. Now I was panicked.

I had been interested in trying a different type of catalyst design for a couple of years. Materials suitable for fabricating the new design were readily available. This was the time to try it. After talking over the idea of using an experimental silver-plated nickel catalyst with rocket engineer Jim McCormick at FMC Corporation, I placed an order for delivery of the nickel screens to our Reaction Dynamics shop in Milwaukee and packed my bags. While I fabricated and assembled the catalyst in Wisconsin, Pete and the crew in Wendover preened the rocket car for its next runs.

The nickel screens were waiting for me when I arrived home. A plating lab in Milwaukee could meet my specification for silver coating the screens and I rushed over to get them started. Afterward, I applied a porous ceramic coating over the plating, using heat treating ovens at a steel fabricating plant in Brookfield, Wisconsin. The hard ceramic prevents damaging erosion of the plating during the heat-generating catalytic decomposition. The next morning, with the new screens in my luggage, I flew back to Salt Lake City. Gerard Brennan met me at the airport and we reassembled the motor back in Wendover.

The morning of Friday, October 9 was chilly, but the action would soon be hot. Gary warmed up the car with a four-second burst. Everything looked and sounded 'right on'. No LNG was available, but we decided to make two test runs on peroxide only. The first was to the north. As the car picked up speed and roared out of sight, Gary inadvertently uncoupled his breathing hose. A check valve blocked the air inlet and he had to drive with one hand steering while holding the valve open with the other in order to breathe - at 462 mph. A return run was made at 478 mph and we then had a two-day wait for the LNG fuel and calm air. Finally, we had something to cheer about.

Gary had found it difficult to see the small USAC mile markers on the course. He needed something more obvious. We decided to erect four by eight-foot plywood sheets on the right side of the course at the beginning and end of the mile speed traps. They were painted green as Gary entered the measured mile and red upon exit, both ways. We found the plywood in Wendover, but the closest paint store was in Wells, Nevada. Some of Gary's friends had discovered a brothel in Wells a few nights earlier. It was late afternoon when we telephoned the store to order the paint, but they were closing soon. So, I used the borrowed business card to call the brothel and asked if someone could do us a favor and collect the paint and brushes to be picked up later that evening. I was told they never closed!

A photojournalist from the German magazine, *Stern*, wanted to interview me over dinner that evening and I obliged him. As our conversation went on longer than expected, I mentioned that I had to go to Wells and pick up the paint. He asked to join me and I continued our interview in the car. When we arrived at this western-style whorehouse he was fascinated with the whole Nevada culture of drinking, gambling, and whatever. I never thought too much about the whole thing until one month later, when the issue of *Stern* with *The Blue Flame* story hit the newsstands. A German-speaking wife of a friend translated the article for me. She was blushing as she returned the magazine and the English translation. He had written at length about our journey to the whorehouse, and left the reader with some very misleading impressions...

At this point the car had made nine full runs, with several peaking at over 500 mph. Although *The Blue Flame* was having its share of teething challenges, it was becoming apparent that it was not the usual LSR vehicle. There had been absolutely no handling problems at any time. Donald Campbell's multi-million-dollar *Bluebird* had required a change in steering ratio. Dr Nathan Ostich's *Flying Caduceus* had persistently veered off course. Art Arfons's *Green Monster* had a penchant for blowing tires. Craig Breedlove's *Spirit of America – Sonic 1* had initially wanted to fly. But *The Blue Flame* was going 'straight-arrow' every run. This was borne out by an almost complete lack of tire wear. The few scuffs visible on one of the tires were from braking in the pits and not the normal high-speed wear from weaving or sliding. In fact, by the end of our stay on the salt, Gary had run the car more than 24 times with more runs over 500 and 600 mph than all of our previous competitors combined. One of the rear tires would remain on for every run. During the entire period no chassis adjustments of any sort were required. That was absolutely remarkable by land speed record standards.

It was now apparent that the only significant challenge would be to develop enough power for long enough to break Breedlove's 600.601 mph record.

The Blue Flame's rocket engine was designed to use catalytically-decomposed 90% concentration hydrogen peroxide as an oxidizer to burn with liquefied natural gas (LNG), which is methane, a cryogenic liquid fuel having a boiling point of -256 degrees Fahrenheit. The LNG was to be directed into the rocket chamber under helium pressure through two injector stages; the first burned 25% of the pre-heated gaseous fuel to increase combustion chamber temperature, then the remainder was injected downstream as a liquid to reach maximum thrust. While peak design thrust was 22,000 lbs, only the first injector stage was intended to be used for these initial subsonic record attempts, yielding 16,000 lbs of thrust. This helped guarantee that the temporary 700 mph speed limit imposed by Goodyear would not accidentally be breached. The rocket could also be run on hydrogen peroxide alone, as a monopropellant system producing 12,400 lbs of thrust. LNG fuel capacity was purposely limited for the subsonic record runs, with a larger fuel tank to be installed later for the anticipated supersonic attempt. After the damaged rocket engine was reconfigured, eliminating the crucial heat exchanger/injectors, maximum thrust attainable was less than 15,000 lbs. *The Blue Flame* would have to set the record with only 90% of its purposely reduced potential power available, and only two-thirds of its ultimate power.

When Pete and I first began working on the rocket car design, we knew our combined engineering research and racing backgrounds would give us a technological advantage. Our ability to communicate design problems to the engineering consultants, and relate the answers to competitive racing situations, resulted in the most phenomenally stable high-speed automobile ever constructed. And now we were responding to new design problems occurring on the salt flats by drawing upon our resource of prior racing experience.

Sunday, October 11, 7:00 am. The red-orange sun barely peeked over the frozen hills ringing the salt as *The Blue Flame* warmed up. Two quick runs were made on straight 90% hydrogen peroxide, the second one at 497 mph. A third run was wasted as I was too excited during refueling and carelessly neglected to reset the LNG throttle valve operator, so the car again ran on peroxide only.

An hour later, the car burned LNG for the first time since September 17. *The Blue Flame* literally rocketed across the salt at 557 mph in the measured mile with the illuminated flaming exhaust trailing. We spotted that the parachute deployment system was slightly singed after the car stopped, so aluminum foil insulation was wrapped around the drogue 'chute lines for protection from the radiating exhaust heat.

I slightly richened the LNG mixture for the next run. Gary blasted off with a spectacular array of iridescent exhaust shock rings following him northbound across the white expanse of Bonneville. Man and car flashed through the mile at 555 mph and disappeared into the mirage under Floating Mountain. To our consternation, USAC observers downrange reported the car wasn't slowing down, no parachutes had been deployed. With the support crew chasing down the track, *The Blue Flame* was not to be seen, just the empty white salt and black center line of dye which defines the course. Finally, three miles beyond the 10-mile International Course, Gary was climbing out of the mud-covered car, which had finally bogged down and slithered to a halt in the salty brine swamp.

Since I had been the last person to attend the stationary rocket car, I was also the last person to arrive on the scene. Zooming down the course at over 100 mph, I nearly got bogged down myself. I saw the *Flame* surrounded by a small crowd of people in front of me, and a line where the white surface suddenly turned tan. It was too late to stop on the hard salt, so I kept the throttle open and threw my car into a wide right-hand slide, 'dirt tracking' an arc around *The Blue Flame* with skidding tires until I was safely back on terra firma. Driving with one hand on the wheel I waved at the surprised onlookers who were waving back.

The problem was that we were now running too rich with the new LNG injectors, so the natural gas was burning outside the tailpipe and had melted the drogue lines. Thus, early Monday found the crew washing off the tenacious mud while we worked with Jim Deist to fabricate heat-resistant aluminum doors for the parachutes. We also fitted smaller injector nozzles to lean out the fuel mixture.

I've heard stories that there was a near mutiny within the team, which Gary quelled, during these difficult periods. Well, I can tell you, the stories were wrong. That word still bothers me. Mutiny implies a change of leadership or defection of the crew, and that surely never happened. That was never the case. There was never a mutiny of any sort.

Instead, I think the word FRUSTRATION captured the mood at the time so much more accurately. After surviving several of these challenges we were becoming exhausted with the tasks at hand and morale was down, tempers short. We had a full team meeting in one of the rooms at the Western Motel and several people vented. Gary talked to the crew but I think Dean Dietrich of IGT, more than anyone, calmed us down and encouraged everyone to push on. I doubt that there's a land speed record team out there that hasn't been through something similar.

On October 13 the LNG injectors were flow-tested and the car was prepared for another run. Power was still lacking, though, as the *Flame* went only 553 mph in the 2,000 ft timing trap on its only try that day.

The following day Gerard welded up right-angle injectors back in Salt Lake City. These would generate a swirling pattern with the LNG to promote better fuel/oxidizer mixing and give it more time to burn completely in the combustion chamber.

Our Milwaukee neighbor, Harley-Davidson, had Denis Manning's motorcycle streamliner out Thursday morning. They cranked off two quick runs averaging 265.492 mph, with Cal Rayborn riding, to set a new world record for motorcycles. This climaxed two weeks of their sorting out handling problems, a few crashes, and various other minor ills. We weren't the only ones learning on the job. I couldn't know it at that very moment, but Reaction Dynamics would return the next year with our piston-engine *Honda Hawk* motorcycle streamliner and go more than 20 mph faster.

Our first run that Thursday saw Gary reach our best speed to date, clocking 581 mph in the kilometer. Lovely iridescent blue exhaust 'diamonds' followed him as he blasted through the timing traps. Once again, I slightly richened the LNG/H2O2 mixture, but then the speed subsequently fell off to 548 mph.

I reset the injectors to the way they were during the first run but since the car was down on power with the jury-rigged injectors, we decided we would now employ the assistance of a push start to get it rolling. Dana Fuller, who had years earlier set a diesel-powered streamliner record at Bonneville, was there watching and offered use of his 'hot rod' Ford van to do it. Fuel saved in overcoming *The Blue Flame*'s starting inertia would be used to thrust it to a higher terminal velocity at the end of the speed traps. By shifting one to two seconds of power from the standing start to the high-speed end of the run, maximum speed could be increased substantially.

After engaging a push bar with the rear suspension, Fuller pushed *The Blue Flame* up to speed. Another car drove parallel, within Gary's view. At a marker cone on the course, the van moved aside and a flagman in the car signaled Gary that all was clear to fire the rocket motor. Then, with a throaty roar the *Flame* quickly disappeared from sight.

Gary could be heard counting off his speeds on the radio as the rocket blasted away from the push car, visibly faster than before. "...450, 500, 550, 600!" As the crew began turning the car around for the return run, we received word that at last we had a leg on the record. Gary had just averaged 609.034 mph.

But he had to make two runs to qualify for the official world land speed record, within an hour of each other. So our joy was suppressed by the chores of refueling, repacking parachutes, checking tires, and repressurizing the compressed air tanks. Just as Gary was preparing to climb back into his 'office', Mike Hopkins, Goodyear's LSR tire engineer, spotted liquid leaking from the nosecone. I placed a drop on my tongue and the stinging sensation immediately indicated peroxide was leaking inside. The record would have to wait as yet another drama unfolded.

With wrenches spinning, the whole crew immediately began removing the nosecone. But before they could pull it free, black smoke wisped out of the body seam. Water was pumped into the front of the car through every opening as news reporters and officials began moving back hurriedly. Finally, the nose piece was removed. Tanks were depressurized. The car was pushed back off the course with its soot-covered innards exposed.

Although everything within the nosecone was covered with black carbon and dry chemical extinguisher powder, damage to the *Flame* was thankfully minimal. Two courageous crewmembers, Mike McCarthy and professional firefighter Dave Bykowski, suffered blisters and minor discomfort from peroxide splashing, but were not really injured. It would be three days before the car would run again.

Sunday, October 18, was sunny and cool. *The Blue Flame* was polished and ready. Heat-damaged air lines had been replaced and pressure tested. A new pressure regulator vent line was rerouted outside the body to prevent a recurrence of Thursday's mishap. After a quick warm-up, the car was poised once again for its race into history. Gary counted down and blasted off again with the blue-tinged exhaust roaring behind him. Over the engine's racket his voice exclaimed: "...500, 550, 600!" This was another record-breaking run! Confident, but understandably wary after our recent disappointments, we prepared for the record-clinching return pass. USAC Chief Steward Joe Petrali drove up and let us know from his expression that it had been a good one: 621.624 mph! Anything near 600 on the return would give us the record.

But suddenly, the gremlins of the salt flats struck again. The main gas pressure regulator began leaking the compressed air which pressurized the peroxide tank. There could be no return run for us that day, either.

Gerard tore down the regulator as he looked for the cause. A speck of dirt in the air pressure lines had caused a minute scratch on the regulator valve seat. Goodyear public relations manager, Dick Ralstin, loaned us toothpaste from his travel case and Gerard lapped and polished the seat. It passed a leak test and was reinstalled.

Time passed quickly and it was late afternoon before the *Flame* was prepared to run again. One hour of daylight was left. Enough for the necessary two runs.

A quick shot northward produced a mile speed of 604.027 mph. The pressure was on again. FIA rules require a new record to exceed the old by at least 1% for official recognition. To reach the minimum required 606.67 two-way average, Gary had to go at least 610 mph coming back.

The sun was peeking low over the mountains and almost blinding us as *The Blue Flame* roared south. Gary climbed out of his seat and waited for Petrali. Pete and I fidgeted and talked confidently. The USAC car drove up. 599.300 mph. A two-way average of only 601.655. One mile per hour over the current mile record but not yet a new one.

We slowly towed the car to the pits. Out of fuel and emotionally drained, seven tired men left their meals half-finished and retired early at the Western Motel that night.

With the previously damaged LNG heat exchanger missing, it was impossible to burn more of that fuel now to increase power. But there still remained one ace to play in the deck! The new silver-plated nickel catalyst pack, which was working flawlessly, was not as temperature-sensitive as the old pure silver one we replaced. Instead of running 90% concentration hydrogen peroxide, we could use a stronger solution, generating more heat and thrust. I quickly called FMC Corporation and ordered several barrels of 90% and 98% peroxide. These would be blended to 94% to give the rocket more punch, hopefully 15,000 lbs thrust, while burning more LNG.

For three days our little Reaction Dynamics team anxiously awaited our H2O2 shipment. The weather was growing worse each day. A winter storm front was moving in from the west when our precious oxidizer finally arrived. Weather reports from the Wendover air base indicated that Thursday would be too windy for us to race. A two-hour break in the weather was expected about 10:00 am Friday, and then all hell would break loose. Old Man Winter was approaching, and fast.

The pre-dawn morning of Friday, October 23 was not inspiring. It was bone-chillingly cold and overcast. Fortified at the Western Cafe against hunger, our determined group left for the race course. It was still windy at 9:30 am, about eight miles per hour. We planned a 10 second warm-up blast to insure a good start. At 10:30 the air suddenly calmed. Gary, already strapped in his seat, accelerated northward on peroxide only, thoroughly heating the catalyst pack, and the tension was broken as the crew leaped into action. When the car came to rest, we were ready to make our two runs for the land speed record. It was time to go racing!

The refueling trucks sped into position and Gary was climbing back into the car at 11:15. As Gary and I went through the checklist, Pete nervously polished the canopy windshield. The repaired LNG regulator loader valve was now leaking slowly. Gary carefully adjusted the pressure. It leaked down again, slowly. "The hell with it, I'll trim it manually", Gary barked. "Let's go!" Pete and I secured the canopy and ran for our cars as *The Blue Flame* was pushed off once more.

"5, 4, 3 ..." the radio blared. Fuller steered his straining van out from behind the rocket and blasted his air horn. The car really looked faster this time, sounded stronger. "...350, 400, 500, 550, 600, 650!" Gary's thrilled voice shouted determinedly over the engine noise. And the speed? 617.602 mph in the flying start mile.

Now for the so-often jinxed second run. Everything had been running so smoothly. What could go wrong this time? Plenty, experience told us. Gary streaked northward on his return at 12.12 pm, his voice calmly rattling off the speeds. It looked like another good run. With its red parachute billowing behind, our beautiful blue and white machine finally slowed to a stop.

"Yeeeeah! We did it!" came over the airwaves from Gary in the cockpit. Our hearts pounded.

Rain began falling gently as Petrali drove up, but we didn't care. Soon the rain would turn into puffy snowflakes, but we didn't care about that, either. The Bonneville season was over, and we were certain that we had just beaten the weather by a hair's breadth. Petrali's beaming face told us that there would be no need for any more races against his electronic chronometers, and then he confirmed it. 627.287 mph for the return run gave us an average of 622.407 mph as the new world record for the mile and 630.388 mph for the kilometer. The new World Land Speed Record was officially 630.388 mph. And it was ours! We were the fastest men in the world! At the very last possible minute, after five weeks of exhausting effort, Craig Breedlove's 600.601 mph had been relegated to history.

The Blue Flame, in two earth-shaking sprints down a 10-mile long stretch of billiard table-flat white crystalline salt, had re-written the history of speed in 3.5485 seconds over the kilometer, 5.784 seconds over the mile. The TV news and press immediately acclaimed the personable Gabelich and *The Blue Flame* as the fastest man and machine on earth – and the first to exceed 1,000 kph!

Gary leaped from the cockpit with his helmet in hand and a brilliant smile as he embraced his father, Mehl. Then, as the USAC boys, our race team, excited spectators and the press gathered around, he held up a hand and said: "Listen! On behalf of myself and the crew, we are dedicating this record to Chuck Suba and his father and mother." Gary, his eyes glistening, then handed Chuck Sr. a photo that he had been carrying on the record runs, an image of a smiling Chuck Jr. in his U.S. Marine Corps uniform. It was a poignant touch.

Gary, the Reaction Dynamics and IGT crew, team members' wives and families, and local hangers-on returned to the Western Motel immediately after addressing the media, in a multi-car parade with our headlights flashing and our horns blaring a staccato cheer. The events of the previous five weeks, and especially the last frantic 24 hours, began to sink into our spinning, sleep-deprived heads. It was an emotional, exhilarating moment for each of us. Cases of champagne suddenly appeared, which we all consumed with gusto.

The telephone in my crowded room rang suddenly; it was a call from the Milwaukee *WTMJ-TV* station sports director, Hank Stoddard. I pulled the phone into a closet, closing the door, so I could hear him over the celebratory din. When he asked me how we felt setting the World Land Speed Record, I shouted "Happy! Everybody's stoned now!" After a brief moment of silence I heard, "Dick, we're on live TV now!"

Pete and Dean and I posed with Gary later for victory photos. Six years of bone-hard labor and preparation, enduring ridicule from skeptics, overcoming frustration and economic hardship had finally won us the World Land Speed Record.

Did we think it was worth it? Gary would naturally reap most of the glory, his due for risking his neck. Our chance for financial gain was lost when the budget ran short and we lost ownership of the car we had slaved to create. But, of course we thought it was worth it, and the goal of a supersonic record still lay before us, a carrot still dangling on a string.

So why did we do it? If you have to ask me that question, you'll never know.

News Item: December 7, 1972 - Apollo 17 launched US scientist Harrison Schmitt and two other astronauts on man's last visit to the lunar surface in the 20th century.

-12-

GARY GABELICH - THRILLSEEKER

Gary's Story in Three Acts
Act One – California Dreamin'

On October 23, 1970 the world excitedly acclaimed Gary Gabelich as the fastest man on earth after he had been the first ever to scream overland at more than 1,000 kph in *The Blue Flame* rocket car.

Thirty years earlier, on August 29, 1940 he had also loudly announced his arrival. His birth, in San Pedro, California, was marked by a loud cry to his beaming parents, Mehl and Raquel Padilla Gabelich. But despite the noise, nobody witnessing the feisty, red-faced, bawling infant in his tiny crib could have predicted the adventurous life he would live.

Attending Long Beach Polytechnic High School after the Gabelich family had moved to Bixby Knolls, Gary began his love affair with high-speed automobiles, pretty typical for a southern Californian teenager in the late Fifties. Borrowing his dad's Pontiac on the sly, he raced it at the Santa Ana dragstrip one day and proudly arrived home with the stock class trophy. Mehl was understandably upset and administered corporal punishment, but was somewhat conflicted; he wanted to admonish his son's disobedience but not to discourage his evident ambition to excel.

Any active young man in southern California at that time would naturally get caught up in the hotrod craze. The radios

Handsome Gary Gabelich in a post-record publicity photo

were resonating with Jan and Dean singing 'Drag City' and 'Little Old Lady from Pasadena' or the Beach Boys' latest hits 'Little Deuce Coupe' and '409'. Every weekend the air was vibrating with the staccato sounds of nitro-fueled Chrysler 'Hemis' at the numerous local drag strips or hotrods burning rubber on deserted suburban boulevards late at night.

Bixby Knolls wasn't exempt from this teenage excitement. Gary's high school buddies were definitely infected by the hotrodding and surfing craze. Bench racing was the topic of discussion at the nearby Grissinger's Drive-In, after school or after work, for these youngsters. Afterwards, impromptu drags were held on Cherry Street near the mausoleum to see who had the right stuff.

Tom 'Mongoose' McEwen was one of Gary's close friends and a fellow Marron Avenue Marauder hotrod club member. "Gary was fearless", he recalls. "You could have offered him a one-way trip to the Moon on a rocket, and he would do it." Gary's favorite stunt was 'street surfing' on a skateboard behind a car on the Long Beach Freeway.

Looking for a less hazardous portal to racing, he began to hang around the neighborhood garages of local drag racers after school and running errands to make himself useful. Lee Vest and Monte Bowers took him along to help one Sunday afternoon at Santa Ana. After watching a couple of nondescript time trial attempts with their Cadillac-powered competition coupe, Gary begged for a chance to try to qualify it. Forging Mehl's required signature on an entry form because he was underage, he hopped in and immediately drove the car faster, hitting over 124 mph. That performance convinced Gary that this was the life of speed he wanted to lead.

Following his 1959 graduation from Long Beach Poly, he found employment at North American Rockwell, starting in the mailroom. Eagerly looking to advance, he moved on to positions as a statistician and then planning engineer. These aerospace industry 'day jobs' were slow-paced compared to his off hours racing escapades. The handsome young Californian with the confident grin was a charismatic driver personality at Lions' Drag Strip, notching frequent wins in a variety of rides.

Imitating jousting knights from the days of chivalry, he began sporting a colorful ostrich plume on his helmet so the fans would recognize his flashy driving style. Later, he began to display the 'dirty digit' flashing past the finish line and earning his nickname, 'The Bone', showing a flare as he dispatched the competition.

By 1962 North American was looking for fit individuals to work as 'stand-ins' for the astronauts on their Apollo program projects. Seeing an opportunity for a more exciting job, Gary jumped at the chance and soon qualified as a test subject. He was immediately engulfed in development activities where he participated in environmental control studies simulating the space environment in the Apollo capsules, such as prolonged high altitude atmosphere, zero gravity, and high G-load re-entry. Eventually, his employer became concerned that his risky lifestyle racing fast cars and boats would imperil their investment in his expensive training. Given an ultimatum, Gary chose the excitement of the race track over space technology.

His racing resume reads like an entry list of prominent Sixties southern California dragsters and drag boats as he became the 'hired gun from Long Beach':

1959 – On April 5, at the San Gabriel dragstrip, the still-teenage Gabelich drove Steve Pick's 'trick' DeSoto hemi-powered dragster, his first 'hot' ride

1961 – *Gary Giblet* – Oldsmobile-powered gas dragster

1961 – Hirshfield and Beaver twin Chevrolet-powered gas dragster

1962 – Hartzler and Steiner twin Chevrolet-powered gas dragster

1962 – *Howard Cams Special* twin Chrysler gas dragster owned by Howard Johansen

1963 – *Valkyrie* jet dragster owned by Bill Fredrick; Gary drove races at Famosa, Bakersfield, and Lions drag strips, and won the first jet car match race against 'Jet car Bob' Smith in Romeo Palamides' *Untouchable*. The *Valkyrie* was also featured in a 1964 movie, 'The Lively Set' with Gary driving a match race against a dragster.

Gary driving the Valkyrie jet dragster at the San Gabriel drag strip

1963 – *Ansen Special*/400 Junior Chevrolet-powered Top Fuel Dragster owned by Bill Martin; Gary drove it the same day he raced against the *Untouchable* in the *Valkyrie*

1965-1966 – *Scoundrel* Chrysler-powered Top Fuel Dragster owned by Sandoval brothers

1965-1967 – *Purple Gang* Chrysler-powered Top Fuel Dragster owned by Rapp, Rossi, and Maldonado

1966 – Thweatt's Automotive Service Fuel Funny Car, *Tweatty Pie*

1967 – Terry Gall's Chrysler-powered Top Fuel Dragster

In the deadly drag boats, Gary's resume was equally impressive and diverse.

1965- *The Ultimate*

1965 – National Drag Boat Association Top Fuel Hydro Championship

1968 – *Climax* B Fuel Hydro, *Citation II* (owned by Rene Andre), *Twister*

1968 – Gary won the national championships in both American Power Boat Association Fuel Hydroplane class and National Drag Boat Association Gas Hydroplane classes – the first person to win both drag boat titles in the same year

Gary racing in the Twister drag boat at 200 miles per hour

*Gary proudly displaying his APBA Fuel Hydro and NDBA Gas
Hydro championships along with his traditional
ostrich-plumed helmet*

Adding further to his southern California lifestyle, Gary
met an attractive young lady, Kathy Foster, in the mid-Sixties.
She was working at the Hollywood Playboy Club as one of the

serving Bunnies. They hit it off almost immediately and were married, although only for a couple years. Each had an exciting career to keep them occupied and so the marriage ended. Kathy later appeared in Playboy Magazine's December 1967 feature, 'The Bunnies of Hollywood'.

Gary's 'thrillseeker' status would be exemplified further by two significant racing events. *Drag News'* Tim Marshall reported this scary saga from Irwindale, California on August 16, 1969: 'With a crowd of 5,479 still watching very closely, Frank Pisano strapped a good hole shot on Gary Gabelich which proved to be just enough as the *Beach City* Vette burst into a ball of fire that just seemed to grow larger and larger. All eyes were on the end of the strip as the large flames were still glowing after the Vette had come to a halt. After a few minutes of mounting tension driver Gabelich was reported in A1 shape as he leaped from the 'still moving' flame engulfed *Beach City* Vette about 100 feet before it came to its final resting place. Needless to say the once beautiful 'candy red' Vette was no more as the burning fiberglass and magnesium could not be put out in time. All Gary could say is, "Thank God for Simpson safety equipment, because of this flame suit I'm still here today!" He only received one small burn on his left leg and stated, "It only feels like bad sunburn." On the run Gary ran an unreal 7.54 to equal Gas Ronda for low ET of the meet but the explosion forced him to shut off with a 175.09 mph leaving 'super sharp' Frank Pisano the winner and Top Fuel Funny Car of the night at a 7.62-183.28.'

On September 14, 1969, just one month after the *Beach City* conflagration, and just weeks before his scheduled land speed attempt, Gary climbed into the *Crisis* Blown Fuel Hydro and set an all-time National Drag Boat Association top speed of 200.44 mph at Lake Perris in California.

This was rather impulsive behavior considering he was contracted to drive *The Blue Flame* in the September-October time frame. But, Gary was not about to sit around waiting for his next thrill.

Act Two – Top o' the World!

I first met Gary at our Reaction Dynamics shop in Milwaukee in December, 1968. He was interested in driving the now retired *X-1* rocket dragster, or another rocket car we might build, and campaign it as an exhibition racer on the west coast. Gary had an extensive racing resume and brought along a scrapbook of his many accomplishments driving funny cars, fuel dragsters, drag boats, and even jet cars. Although we had no intention of racing a rocket again on the drag strips we were impressed by his clean-cut appearance, eagerness, and varied experiences. We didn't want to run the *X-1* again and so had nothing to offer him, but little did we know how soon our paths were to cross once again.

The American Gas Association planned the announcement of the land speed record project with a press conference at the Beverly Hills Hotel on May 1, 1969. After interviewing a shortlist of prospective drivers, we had come to an agreement with my good friend and renowned dragster driver, Don Garlits, to pilot *The Blue Flame*. However, due to family pressures, Don had changed his mind at the 11th hour. After working around the clock to re-write all of the press releases and revise the format, the press conference took place on schedule without a driver being named.

Gary's fateful Milwaukee visit a few months earlier had occurred after our original selection process was completed. Now, once again reflecting on our driver options, we realized that he was the perfect choice if he would agree. His experience driving a large variety of vehicles and boats made him a fast study in high-performance machines. This would be the type of quick adaptation needed to control our rocket-powered extreme machine, *The Blue Flame.*

I called Gary that afternoon after the press preview and visited him in Long Beach the next day. He signed a letter of intent to accept the driving challenge on May 2. I sent him a driver agreement rough draft on May 7 so we could begin negotiations. The initial contract was agreed to and signed on June 27, so with an advance bonus Gary and Reaction Dynamics were now a team, optimistically planning to be on the salt flats in the September-October timeframe. That goal was way too optimistic as it turned out.

On July 29 it became apparent our schedule was in jeopardy, so we informed Gary of the slippage with the intent of still going later in 1969. Finally, on October 25 the AGA announced that our record attempt would be postponed until the fall of 1970. On December 20 Gary and Reaction Dynamics agreed on a new contract. However, that would soon become moot as *The Blue Flame* ownership devolved to the Institute of Gas Technology since we had missed our original contracted date.

Gary visited our Milwaukee shop a few times in 1969 so we could work out the locations of instruments and controls as well as fit the upholstery to his anatomy. In a neat touch it was sewn by Chuck Suba's dad. Gary worked very closely with our busy crew of fabricators and the whole Reaction Dynamics gang enjoyed his companionship on these brief occasions.

He also made several publicity appearances to promote the project in 1970 for the American Gas Association while the car was being finished. Finally, *The Blue Flame* debuted at the

Southern Gas Association conference at Houston's Astroworld Park on April 29. Gary's appearance there helped spark renewed gas industry interest in funding the land speed record runs and pushed financing for the project budget over the top.

At last, the week of July 27, Gary and *The Blue Flame* were united for the initial static testing at the Great Lakes Dragaway in Union Grove, Wisconsin. With the *Flame* tethered to a steel post sunk 12 ft into the ground in the track's pit area, the rocket engine roared to life. Following a few adjustments back at the Reaction Dynamics shop, on September 4 the design power was achieved. Finally, *The Blue Flame* was towed down the dragstrip at 80 mph so that Gary could make a quick check of the steering and brakes before final preparations began for the road trip to Utah.

While Gary was fun-loving and carefree working with the crew on the Salt Flats, once he climbed into *The Blue Flame* a different man emerged. He was all business. Even back in our shop in Milwaukee he would constantly fiddle with the cockpit controls, mentally preparing for both the routine and the unexpected events that might ensue. I drew him a labeled diagram of *The Blue Flame*'s instrument panel and he spent an hour every night in Wendover's Western Hotel rehearsing his operation of the controls and emergency situation countermeasures.

This studious approach paid dividends for Gary when high-speed challenges suddenly appeared at Bonneville. He confronted them with a calm and calculated response worthy of any test pilot. Listening to his radio monologues (we had one-way communication to avoid distraction) it sounded like he was reading a script even when there were emergency situations. This wasn't the 'wild man' drag racing persona from southern

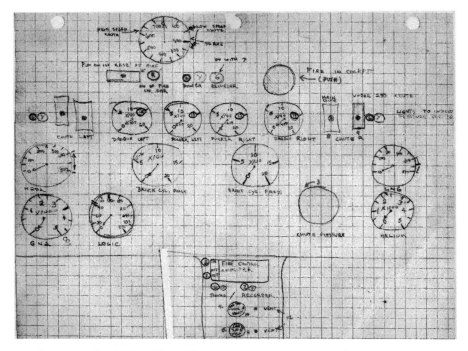

Gary studied The Blue Flame instrument panel diagram nightly

California we had read about in *Drag News*. On the final run for the record, Gary drove *The Blue Flame* with one hand while he manually adjusted the LNG tank pressure with the other – at over 600 mph!

One big mistake would ultimately temper his triumph, however. He never came to a contract agreement with the Goodyear Tire & Rubber Company. As a result, Gary's name was erased in all the Goodyear advertising that followed the record. That also foreclosed any possible future sponsorship for his projects.

Then, after a busy year promoting his world record-setting status, worldwide media appearances on behalf of the natural gas industry, and a USO visit to the troops in Vietnam, 'thrillseeker' Gary returned.

218

Act Three – Triumph or Tragedy?

As the excitement of the World Land Speed Record began to fade, Gary commissioned Paul Sutherland's Race Car Works to build him a new ride, a Vega panel truck four-wheel-drive Chrysler-powered rear-engine funny car for dragstrip exhibition appearances.

This project initially began during discussions between Bob Kachler and Kenny Youngblood at Kachler's Racing Graphics office in Long Beach. After concept drawings were prepared, chassis-builder Sutherland became involved along with engineer Al Willard who had experience with monocoque race car design on Can-Am sports racers. Kachler had known Gary since the mid-Sixties, helped promote his various drag race ventures, and discussed this project with him. Gary believed that dragstrip exhibitions would be a lucrative income source and agreed to help fund the project, lending his name to the car.

The result was a monocoque chassis with full suspension and a fiberglass Vega panel truck body covering the works. But because the concept was so unusual, the project dragged on for almost 12 months while Paul and Al designed and fabricated all of the unique components that comprised this technical tour de force. Gary and Kachler raised some sponsor money from NGK and Valvoline but Gary was heavily committed financially as well. As it came together, his cadre of racing friends converged and lent their skills, including Gary Scow who helped with fabrication, Don Kirby (*Beach City* Corvette) who provided the paint job and Roy Richter (Cragar Industries) who built the custom wheels. Ed Pink also collaborated, building the blown Chrysler Hemi powerplant.

Gary discussing his 4-wheel-drive exhibition funny car with the CRAGAR sponsor

After several false starts to test the car, finally on April 7, 1972 it all came together at the Orange County International Raceway dragstrip. Monogram Models had agreed to come in as a sponsor at the last moment and wanted publicity photos to promote the proposed model of the dramatic-looking car. Gary and the Vega had not turned a wheel under power until now. The tests and photo shoot were scheduled for a non-race day at the track, so no safety crew or ambulance was present.

That day at Orange County, Gary's racing career, and life, nearly ended. Paul Sutherland recalls the fateful outing. "The Ed Pink motor was running too rich at warm-up, so we leaned it out. Gary was to make just a short burnout, half track, for some publicity photos and then we would begin sorting out the car. He was broke by then, so when the Monogram rep told him he'd give him $5,000 if he smoked the tires the full track for his photographers, his eyes opened wide." Not known for doing things by halves, this was all the incentive Gary needed to let it all hang out.

"Gary nailed it and never lifted," Sutherland continued. "He just drove it to the right side of the track, hitting the high-mounted Armco barrier, then the support post, and then it veered left into the other guardrail, hitting the posts, which split the car in half at the monocoque. Gary and the chassis then slid under the Armco which began slicing the car and him. He hit his head and split his helmet open."

Gary himself recalled: "I tried to undo my seat belt and I couldn't get it undone with my left hand so I pulled down my goggles with my right hand. My left hand was laying down where my left elbow is. It was hanging by a few tendons and some skin, like a wet dishrag.

"Then I realized my left leg wasn't where it was supposed to be. It was alongside of my body, kind of crumpled up in a weird way. I knew I was really messed up."

When the stunned crew reached the burning wreckage, Gary was tangled up in the rollcage with his left hand torn almost completely off and his legs mangled into shapeless appendages. Rather than wait for an ambulance, Scow and Sutherland gently placed him in the rear of their Chevy station wagon. Racing on to the freeway, they realized they didn't know where the nearest hospital was and pulled off on the second exit in Tustin, seeking directions. A passerby pointed down the street and yelled "There!"

As they carried Gary into the Tustin Community Hospital ER, a hospital staff member immediately paged a surgeon who was leaving, having just replaced a man's severed thumb. The surgeon rushed back and quickly had Gary wheeled into the operating room. Nine hours later, he was patched up and made whole again. His left leg had also been broken in 15 places and was mended with steel rods. This was the beginning of a lengthy hospital stay and series of operations to complete the repairs.

Reliving the event, Sutherland opines, "Gary always had the reputation of never backing off in a race car or boat. It's likely the problem started because smoke from the front tires filled the closed cockpit so he couldn't really see the track ahead clearly and he just stayed on it, crashing at almost 200 mph."

"At first the doctors told me I might be lucky to regain 65 per cent use of my left hand," Gary recalled six months later. "But look. I have more than that, probably 85 per cent. Some of the nerve endings are gone and I've lost some of the feeling, but it's part of me, not a hook.

"I have a steel rod running into my left heel. I almost lost the leg a couple of times when gangrene developed, but they were able to clean it up. It's bent all out of shape - mostly to the left – but that means I'll be able to run around left-hand corners real fast."

He was philosophical about the accident, and used the downtime to ponder his latest project, a rocket-powered machine that would challenge the sound barrier. It would be an evolution of *The Blue Flame,* to be called *The American Way*. "I want to live as much as the next guy, probably more so because I enjoy what I'm doing," he said. "But I'd just be a vegetable if I was forced to quit. You have to be a driver to understand what I'm talking about. Besides, I've paid my dues, now. I've been injured about as badly as one man can and lived. I figure it can't happen twice."

My co-author David Tremayne remembers meeting Gary at Black Rock Desert in 1983, during *Thrust2*'s final successful attempt on our record.

"He was a cool dude, a typically laid-back Californian. I knew his story, and liked him immediately. From the way he walked and handled himself you'd never have guessed what lengthy and painful rehabilitation he must have gone through after that shunt. Richard Noble and I partnered in a game of pool against Gary and his friend Van one night in Bruno's Country Club in Gerlach. Damaged hand or not, Gary and Van won…"

I last met Gary at Bonneville, during a weekend of record setting with Tony Fox's Pollution Packer rocket dragster in October, 1972. Tony had invited Gary, the reigning world record holder, along with Craig Breedlove and Art Arfons, to enjoy a weekend of FIA-sanctioned acceleration record setting. After Dave Anderson and Paula Murphy drove the rocket-powered dragster to records in the ¼-mile, 500 meters, and the kilometer, a party ensued at a dude ranch outside Wendover in Nevada that evening. While a cowboy band sang to entertain the crowd, Gary, who was still recovering from his Vega crash, ceremoniously announced his recovery by throwing one of his crutches into the bonfire. Was the 'thrillseeker' back once more?

The hairy drag boat rides were still available. Just like his early days on the drag strips, Gary jumped into a parade of high-powered and dangerous drag boats. His favorite was Peggy Brendel's *Shockwave II*, later renamed *Aftershock*.

Again, bad luck intervened and he almost met his end on Nevada's Turlock Lake in 1975 when his Western Mag blown fuel hydroplane drag boat, *Pandemonium* went airborne and destructed completely while thundering over the water at more than 180 mph. As he was ejected from the catapulting hull, the engine hit him squarely in the back with resulting severe injuries to his liver and kidney. Recovery this time included months of weekly visits to a kidney dialysis clinic.

His career as a speed merchant seemed stalled after the boat accident. His friend, Tom Daniel, thought it might be time to put together a marketing business, Rocketman Productions, Inc., to help promote Gary as the World Land Speed Record holder and organize another attempt to build the stillborn $500,000 supersonic rocket-powered car. Tom was an inventive artist and illustrator with connections in the model car industry. Gary was named president of the company, with Tom as executive vice president, his new wife Rae (Gary had married Rae Ramsey in January 1978) was secretary-treasurer, Dan Bisher handled corporate communications. Doug Kruse came on board with engineering expertise to input into the design of the new car.

"I first met Gary in the late Sixties when I was living in East LA and came down to watch him driving 'diggers' (slingshot dragsters) at Lions Drag Strip in Wilmington," recalls Tom. "That was some time before he drove *The Blue Flame* and set the world record. We became close friends and, eventually, business partners. We collaborated on the new land speed record vehicle design, *The American Way*, over several years, planning to push the record over 800 mph." Tom built a scale model and began promoting the project with the motor sports contacts from his industrial design career. The design was finally completed in 1983. "I still get chills just looking at it. It still looks like it could do the trick today."

A year later these aspirations would come to an abrupt end. "Our hopes and dreams were prematurely shattered with Gary's tragic death on January 26, 1984. He was riding his Harley out to a cliff on the Pacific Coast Highway where we used to go to discuss our future ventures. A furniture van turned abruptly in front of him. The lift gate was sticking out horizontally behind and Gary's head struck it. He was conscious in the hospital for a while but died after a few hours. He smiled at Rae one last time, then passed on."

In a manner somewhat reminiscent of T.E. Lawrence at the conclusion of 'Lawrence of Arabia', Gary achieved his zenith as a handsome young hero at the age of 30. Both had conquered life-threatening challenges and achieved world acclaim with

Gary and his ill-fated Harley Sportster motorcycle

cheerful aplomb and a keen focus on success. His bright star of fame was dimming in his mid-forties, and like Lawrence on his Brough Superior SS100 motorcycle, he similarly abruptly met his Maker while riding his Harley-Davidson to watch the red-orange sun setting over the Pacific horizon. Beatle George Harrison wrote these lyrics for triple World Champion Jackie

Stewart, but they applied equally to Gary, lost that chilly January day:

Faster than a bullet from a gun
He is faster than everyone
Quicker than the blinking of an eye
Like a flash you could miss him going by
No one knows quite how he does it but it's true they say
He's the master of going faster.

-13-

GERARD BRENNAN – THE ALTERNATE DRIVER

Gerard Brennan's name remains displayed beneath that of Gary Gabelich on the side of *The Blue Flame*, just by the cockpit window. Had anything happened to the former, he would have been the alternative driver, the man who might have set the last land speed record for America. But he did a lot more than have his name on the side of the rocket car, having become associated with the project early in the game.

"I was a partner with Chuck Suba. He was the Pied Piper of speed in Evanston and he and his partner Gene Burcham and I started building a car. I first met Chuck when he was going over a 471 supercharger for a guy from the North shore. The guy's bugging him, asking him questions and leaning over his shoulder all the time and Chuck looked over at him – and this is like a $150, $200 job that he's gonna knock out in a coupla hours, and that was fantastic money back then, a lot of money, and he says to the guy: 'You got your shoes on?' And the guy says, 'Yeah,' kind of uncertainly. And Chuck says, 'Well, take a walk!' Chuck was a character, different!

"He was doing Precision Engines when I met him, and as a club nine of us in 1959 or '60 had bought a '53 Henry J and we were gonna run this X Class, which was any American four cylinder engine. The car had a Flathead in it, and we started talking about it to Chuck and Gene, and Chuck said 'Why don't you buy this Model A and convert it to overhead valve? A friend

Gerard Brennan, alternate driver, and valued Reaction Dynamics team member

of mine has it on the North Shore with a three-speed synchromesh transmission. Don't waste time with the Flathead.' So that's what we did. We called it the Brennan-Frankie Special, because my partner's second name was Frankie. That got us in the door with Chuck, to where you didn't have to throw your hat in to see if it was gonna come flying back out.

"At that time Chuck and Gene were just completing a Top Fuel car, made out of exhaust tube. Then he sold that and decided to build another car and include me in, so I was a partner in it. Then he buys Gene out of the car and the machine shop because he's going to the South side and unbeknown to me he's selling everything on the North side. So I bought a race car without an engine from him and then I bought his '59 Chrysler Imperial as a tow car. Then he slid into a partnership on the South side in a Fuel Coupe with Jake Schuljak, and eventually he was gonna go jet car racing. Then, when he was in the midst of doing all that, Dick Keller came down and got him interested in the *X-1*.

"Then on a Sunday afternoon I'm at the lakefront watching drag racing on a pond down there, and I don't know how I found out because this is before cell phones, but before I left that day I knew that Chuck had been killed driving someone else's car."

Curiously, Brennan never saw the *X-1* run, "But I took a ride from them by invitation when it went to Detroit when they put it in the new car show."

His own claim to fame in drag racing was to be The Man Who Missed The Sixes. It seemed he could never break into the six second bracket for elapsed times, but there was a good reason for that. "I never ran a six in my life. I got into the sevens, then I would go down to a smaller class car and get that down to the bottom of the sevens. Then I got in Dick's *Pollution Packer* rocket car in 1975 and did a short blast and ran a 7.40 or something, then I went 5.5 and four, running it at Union Grove. We were low e.t. of the meet. It was raining the Friday night so I couldn't run then and that was good with me, I was perfectly happy that I didn't have to run then, because I'd rather make my first run in a rocket car in the daytime. In Fuel drag racing with wheel drive, you couldn't let your head touch the headrest because it'd vibrate your eyes out of your head. On the thrust car, you couldn't hold your head off of it. You figure out that there's no chance of that, so you might as well put it against there right from the start. It was probably pulling 5g in the middle of the track. That was how I went straight from the sevens to the fives, and missed out the sixes altogether."

Gerard joined *The Blue Flame* program because of Pete Farnsworth, whom he knew well from the drag racing scene. "By the time I got there they had the beam [the main part of the jig on which the chassis was built to ensure that that it was in true alignment] and the bulkheads were standing up and they had the longerons in. Pete had called me. I had met him at Union Grove, and he'd been a good friend of Chuck's. The really strange thing is that the Henry J was Leah Farnsworth's dad's car, so when we showed up with the Flathead in it one time at a dragstrip she came over and introduced herself asked where we'd got the car. There were only a handful of 53s. She and Pete were running a Fuel car and we were only in Bracket X, but right away we were chatting all the time with the Farnsworths, the big guys up there with the Fuel car! Pete was a real nice guy, a real straight shooter."

Gerard did a lot of the welding and fabrication on the *Flame* as the build process continued.

"I did somewhere around 60 percent of the aluminum, and Kenny McCarthy did the full front suspension. When we got to building the suspension – and we started both the front and the rear around the same time and each had the drawings of what they were gonna be – we had one welding machine. We had a Miller heli-arc machine which we did all the arc welding with. We had no wire welding equipment. We started on the front suspension and I was working with Pete on the rear suspension, setting up all the angles. I did the machine work on all the milling for the rear tubes and Kenny got ahead of me welding on the front suspension.

"By that point they'd asked me if I would be the alternate driver, which gave me one hell of an advantage over everybody because I could talk to Paul Torda, I could talk to Carl Uzgiris. So I said to Kenny, 'Why don't you just do the whole front suspension? If somebody sends me over here, which would only be Pete, to weld on this, I'm gonna refer him to you. And I'll do the full rear suspension. That way there won't be any of this kind of nonsense going on. So that's what we did.

"When I showed up in Milwaukee I'd just driven a Top Fuel car a week before, 215 out of Rockford with it, but that car wasn't gonna go anywhere anymore because we'd been rained out of so many meets that the person who owned the car was going broke. The County Mountie was looking for him to have an auction on the car! So I went up there and Keller gave me the tour of the shop. There was no nosecone for the car, they'd built the jig, they didn't have the fuel tank, the engine wasn't there, it was still being made. It may have been made already but whatever pot and pan company made it sent it to Milwaukee which was a stellar mistake. Ray Dausman should have been over there watching them make it and looking over their shoulders, and he was back here running his calculator, making numbers. So it showed up and he didn't like the finish on the engine so they shipped it back to be redone. The only one problem with that is now they don't know where they're at when they go to put it in a lathe to turn things, because they'd lost all their marks on the casing. So the back of the motor ended up awful thin and they welded plugs in so they could bolt a smaller cone in if they needed a smaller nozzle. And one of those pooped it on the Salt Flats and cracked, and I got to weld that up.

"There was supposed to be a deep fairing at the front, deep to the salt, but we didn't have time to build it. We had time to build a big tailfin that was too tall for supersonic, and canard wings on it which were only for supersonic. They had no effect subsonic. If time is money, then we wasted both. The vertical stabilizer just took a lot more time to build if it was twice as high as what we needed.

"I asked Dick, 'What are these on here for, if they're supersonic and Goodyear says their tires have a speed limit on them of 700 which is well under the speed of sound as far as the vehicle is concerned...' He said they were on there for "political lift", whatever that was!"

At Bonneville, besides being the back-up driver should anything happen to Gary Gabelich, Gerard's duties included refueling which was potentially as dangerous. He never got to drive the *Flame*, "But I operated the engine at Union Grove, with the car tied down. That was long before I drove *Pollution Packer*. Gary had tried it once, then we did a full-thrust run with the *Flame*, and you could feel and hear a lot of stuff going on behind you! All the fuel charging by you, 2000 pounds of fuel flowing in 22 seconds... Really hauling butt. And it weighs 12 pounds a gallon, so it made a helluva noise as it goes by you. I welded all the fuel lines together and put all the couplings on, so I'm sitting there thinking, 'Don't split a fuel line now!'"

Gerard gives a wry laugh when he remembers the time on the salt. "Hmm, yeah! The whole thing took a lot longer than anyone thought. We thought we were gonna be there for a week or two. You know, we didn't even have a tent to work in. You wore a hat, that was your protection from the sun. There was no big entourage.

"One time, when we got into the high 500s, we ran in the rain. We got it all ready to go, and it starts raining. We really didn't have the ability to take the peroxide back outta the car, other than to run it out. Everyone's looking around, 'What do we do?' Well, let's run... So they called Joe Petrali and said, 'We're gonna make a pass.' And he said, 'Well, it's raining out here.' And we said, 'Yeah, but it's not windy. We don't care.' So we wiped the top of the fuselage off all the way right to the front of the car so he wouldn't have all this water coming back at him, and we made a pass. Joe's says, 'Well, we'll put this down as a test run.' They're all tests runs until you're backing up your record!"

Apart from the problems associated with developing the new engine technology, there were very few with The *Flame* itself. They only had to change three of the Goodyear tires in the 27 runs that they made, and they lost a couple of braking parachutes.

"The thing with one tire was that it got flat-spotted. One of our crew members got in harm's way while Gary was standing in the cockpit after a run, steering the car. We never formulated a program of how we were gonna stop! He was standing in the car and the crew was on the pick-up truck which was towing him. One member got off and we were trying to figure how to stop Gary without him running into the tow vehicle. The guy tried to untie a knot in the nylon towline. Well, how're you gonna untie a knot in that when you've been pulling a 6000 pound car out of soft salt? I don't think you're gonna get that knot out of there, maybe ever. So we waved to Gary that he was gonna have to stop, in kind of a panic mode, and he stood on the pedal and locked a rear tire. Didn't get the other one, though, and that stayed on all 27 runs.

"With the 'chutes, first of all we had a problem when we couldn't get any parachutes out because we burned everything off the back of the car. Then we put doors on the back to stop that.

"Then we were losing the 'chutes because the air speed indicator was wrong. We were losing them going from the high-speed 'chute to the low-speed one because we were doing that at too high a speed. We didn't know how to check and prove the air speed indicator, and we were getting a low reading because the lines on the pressure side were loose. While the car was down having some other work done we took the pitot tube off and took the air speed indicator over to the Wendover Airbase and they were kind enough to test it for us. They said it was inaccurate at the low numbers by a couple miles an hour and at the real high numbers, but around 600 to 700 it was almost spot-on. That was really interesting how they tested it, because they put a balloon in it and it should register 60 mph or something. Okay, so we get back and put the balloon on the air speed indicator, and the balloon was empty. So we pulled all the hatches off and tightened all the couplings, and then we got that reading and we stopped losing parachutes, because we'd been going about 100 mph faster than we thought when we were deploying them before.

"So then we set a record one-way but the car caught on fire. So we put a regulator vent line in the nose so that we wouldn't get a repeat of the problem. Then we went faster than the previous record by one percent but we had damaged the regulator. I surmised that it might have been a little chip of stainless steel that came in or out of one of the hoses, which chipped the regulator going through it at high velocity, and I rebuilt that myself. One of the writers had his kit with him and I lapped it in using his toothpaste! That solved that.

"On the final runs we picked up a lot of speed because we went to the 98 percent peroxide. They got 50 percent off the

234

price of the 90 percent strength peroxide, and that was a real sweet deal. We had a railroad car full of it, but then they needed some hotter stuff, 98 percent military peroxide and that came by truck because they wouldn't fly it as it was too corrosive. I don't remember how many barrels they got, but we would use two per run.

"We didn't use the pure 98 percent stuff on its own because that would have been too hot for the catalyst pack; we blended it with the 90 percent stuff. We were putting two barrels of 90 with one of 98, to bring that up to about 92/93, but not over 94. We got at least another 100 mph."

"I've heard lots of stories, usually emanating from Europe, that the LNG never got used. Bullshit! We used it, no question."

Gerard is also adamant that airflow over parts of *The Blue Flame* was supersonic on the record run.

"When the car picked up speed the tires stood up, like any tires would, and got narrower and deeper in the salt. And on both record runs I say we had supersonic air infringement under them, and nobody wanted to recognize that. The salt was clean on every run apart from the last two. The tires blew pieces of salt out of the tracks. In the record there was a false time, and Joe Petrali writes as explanation of that the loose flying salt produced a double trip of the clocks. The higher speed broke the upper surface of the salt off and sucked it into the air. We weren't going supersonic, but some of the airflow was. They called out 650 mph as clear as a bell on the first run, and around that speed the airflow is certainly transonic."

Gerard gives a rueful laugh at mention of the tensions on the Salt Flats. "Hah! I don't want to go into detail because it was private. But it came to head when somebody asked a question that shouldn't have been asked, in my book. And it was answered wrong, totally wrong, and agreed by three of the team members. And they were being told that they could get a Greyhound bus and go home. Well that would have scrapped the record. We didn't have team back-up, we'd been there four weeks, we weren't suddenly gonna again start from scratch. I think about then we may have been faster than the record but couldn't back it up. I said that because we were a team, it should be all of us at the curb getting a Greyhound bus. Not just three people who mis-spoke. What we needed was the three people who spoke out to apologize and hope like hell that the person who asked the question would accept the apology so that we could move on.

"The other thing that kinda frosted my cookies a little bit was the fact that it looks and sounds like, if you listened to these guys at the Salt Flats, that the record went from one guy in California right to the English guys. It skipped us. But that's totally typical of Breedlove. I hate to even say his name. He's a self-centered son-of-a-bitch, to make it mild.

"Gary screwed us real good by not signing a contract with Goodyear. If he had, there would have been a hell of a lot more recognition of what *The Blue Flame* did. They would have spent a million dollars or more on making his name and *The Blue Flame* name a household word across the country. Which is what happened to Breedlove. Breedlove blew all kinds of smoke up Gary's butt, and Gary didn't sign. He was asking for a million dollars, because Breedlove said they gave him a million dollars. I told him straight out, before we even went to the salt, 'Gary, there's no way! They may have given him a million dollars *overall*, but they passed the record back and forth with Firestone how many times, Gary? Does Breedlove have a beautiful 'shop out there in California? Yes he does. But that's not where he came from. He came out there with his own car, he also built another one.'

"Don Garlits was the first choice, but by the time I was hired on the crew we already knew it was Gary. They'd their 1969 presentation press conference in California and they thought they were going there to say Garlits, and he turned them down. His idea was a great one, he was gonna consider it like a very long drag race.

"The other thing that gets me, Gary gets on TV, on the Johnny Carson Show, and all he could talk about was Breedlove. A few years later, Breedlove's got a supersonic car mock-up and *he's* on the Johnny Carson Show. Doesn't mention *The Blue Flame* at all, doesn't mention Gary...

"People ask me what was Gary like? It's a good question... Hah! I don't know what other people's experience of him was, but no matter what I told him, he wouldn't argue. I never told him in the middle of the day that it was midnight. But I would tell him things that I thought were perfectly logical, against what he was asking Dietrich to do, and he'd sit there and shake his head, yeah, and then he just did what he was already doing.

"The insurance policy... Same money as he was being given to drive the car. I told him they'd give him half that money gladly, to not have the insurance and to cash you out of the insurance thing that's in your contract. I said, 'What is the point? The first thing, do you really think you're gonna buy the ranch?' Because I don't think he would get in the car - I know I wouldn't - if he thought that. I didn't plan on meeting my maker on the Salt Flats. And he *would not* argue. He'd just shake his head, 'Yeah, yeah.' Like I was right. I told him, 'It's a real big pain in Dietrich's ass to try to get this insurance, and you've got in your contract that you have to have it.' Well, some of the things he had in there were good. When he was driving, we had to have a doctor out there. That was cool. But the insurance... I said, 'They'll give you half the money for the insurance, they'll write you a check right now. Get it off Dietrich's shoulders. You take that and you put it in a joint account with your Mom. If you buy the ranch at the salt they are not gonna expect your people to put you in the ground, the gas industry will cough up the rest of the loot to do a nice thing for you. So that's not coming out of your Mom's money, and she's got half the money that she woulda got, but you weren't expecting to have to give it to her anyway.' And he goes right back to Dietrich and says, 'I have to have the insurance.' He had already made up his mind, and wouldn't argue.

"Gary had very little or no engineering knowledge, whatsoever. I've said it before and I'll say it again: Gary would ride a five liter jerry can with a Bic lighter, if he thought it woulda made him fast and famous. He didn't need the engineering. He was happy to ride on someone else's engineering. He was happy to be a hired gun.

"After the record we were gonna build two quarter mile rocket cars, because he was The Rocketman. I was supposed to drive one, he was supposed to drive the other one. We were supposed to tour the country, but not together. Gary would go one way, I'd go the other. I'd go to a track, break the record, then when he got to that track he'd break that record. All for show. He got his money and his fame, then he had his friends in California build him an all-wheel drive Funny car, some kind of Chevy panel wagon body. He put all his money in that.

"We were up in Milwaukee and he went out to the 225-mile race at the fairground, which always followed the Indy 500, and I met up with him there. He'd got this beautiful book of his new show car. I'd like the money he just spent on that! He opened it up and there it is. He flicks me through it. Now we're down to the last page and looking at the chassis itself, and I said to him: 'Where's the centre of the wheelbase?' And he said, 'It's right there, behind the driver's head.' And I said it was in the wrong place. 'You need to have more wheelbase.' But they still built it the way it was laid out and he had a real bad accident where he stuffed it into one guardrail and then into the other guardrail. Hurt himself big time."

For two years after the record was broken, Gerard went on tour with *The Blue Flame*.

"I didn't get drafted to 'Nam because of my asthma so I never thought I'd get out of the country, but this was my ride out. We took the car to Europe and had a month off out there. We took the pick-up truck and went for a ride down to Rome, we roamed around Europe, a little bit in France, which was very cool."

-14-

JOE PETRALI – LEGENDARY TIMEKEEPER

Of the many persons I came in contact with on the LSR project, perhaps none was more interesting than Joe Petrali. Joe was the United States Auto Club (USAC) Chief Steward for our timing record attempts at the Bonneville Salt Flats. At that time the Automobile Competition Committee for the United States (ACCUS-FIA) was the national sanctioning body recognized by the Federation Internationale de la Automobile for all auto racing in the United States. USAC was a member organization of ACCUS-FIA and designated to time and certify certain (international and world) automobile records for the FIA.

Although I had several years' experience in drag racing, I had none in land speed record setting at Bonneville. So, at the advice of USAC headquarters, in the summer of 1968 I traveled to meet Joe at his office in LaVerne, California. My objective was to learn whatever I could about the various requirements for setting international and world records under FIA sanction. At that meeting I also began to learn about a fascinating and legendary individual, Joe himself.

The first hint of what this man was about came when I commented on a black and white photograph hanging on his office wall. "Joe, is that you in that picture with Howard Hughes?" I asked. He grimaced and nodded yes. "Joe, is that plane you are standing on the *Spruce Goose*?" "Actually, it's the Hughes Flying Boat" was his quiet response. "Howard never liked it being called the *Spruce Goose*."

241

We then discussed the LSR project and how we wanted to attempt a world land speed record in September, 1969. Joe gave me lists of names to contact at the State of Utah Bureau of Land Management in Salt Lake City, the Western Motel in Wendover, and said he would handle the paperwork with USAC, ACCUS-FIA and the FIA in Paris, France.

Joe Petrali and Howard Hughes discussing the controversial "Spruce Goose" flying boat

I took him out to lunch and pestered him some more about that famous airplane and pilot. He was reluctant about it, but I extracted a small part of the story of that famous moment in the Long Beach, California harbor when the Hughes Flying Boat (*Spruce Goose*) flew for the first and only time – with Joe as the flight engineer. The rest of that saga I learned seven years later in a February 1975 TRUE magazine story, written posthumously. Joe, who died of a heart attack in 1973, would never reveal his relationship with Hughes while he lived. But that wasn't the whole story about the remarkable Joe Petrali.

As I continued to ask him questions about running on the salt flats and the course layout, his eyebrows suddenly raised and he had a smile on his face. "Let me get this straight now", he said, "you and your crew have never even been to the Bonneville Salt Flats, right?" I nodded affirmatively.

"And you intend to go out there next year and break Craig Breedlove's World Land Speed Record, right?" Again I nodded.

"You do know his record is 600 mph!" "Yes", I replied.

"You do know that you have to go at least 607 mph to set a new record?" he continued. "That's what it says in the FIA rulebook, exceed the record by 1%." I again responded by nodding my head.

"Well, then, we'll have to help with your education", Joe said, chuckling.

He then suggested that I witness land speed racing first hand later that summer. Mickey Thompson planned to publicize the new 1969 Ford Mustang Mach 1 pony car by setting numerous FIA international speed and endurance records at Bonneville on the International Course. Joe and his USAC crew would be out there timing and certifying the records, so he invited me to witness the event.

I flew from Chicago into Salt Lake City airport on September 9, 1968, rented a car and drove west on the straight, level 125-mile stretch of US40 to the Utah/Nevada state line at Wendover, arriving in the evening. After checking into the historic Western Hotel, I walked over to the diner and found Joe and his timing crew finishing dinner. He told me to eat quickly and get some sleep as the fun would be starting at sunrise.

The next morning I jumped up suddenly as a rooster crowed outside my window, waking me up. Then I drove east on the highway out of town and on to the salt (which I had promised the Avis girl would not happen). Mickey had set up an encampment with all of his Mustangs and service equipment near the mile six marker and off to the side of the course. He also had a double-wide trailer (a ranch house, really) parked opposite the USAC timing trailer.

Inside the timing trailer, Joe and his crew fired up their generator and warmed up the timing lights, electronic timers, etc. They were to be out there for two weeks as Mickey and Hawaiian racer Danny Ongais set over 100 records for speed and distance on the international straight line course and the 10-mile circle course for class B (305 to 488 cu in) and class C (183 to 305 cu in) sedans.

As the Mickey Thompson team prepared the various Mustangs for their record runs there was plenty of down time for Mickey and the USAC crew. Joe introduced me to Mickey later in the day. "Mick, here's a young man who will be coming out here next year to break Craig's record." Mickey looked me over carefully, and then exclaimed: "You'd better have a ton of money if you want to do that." "We do," I boasted. Then Mickey looked over toward one of the Mustangs and said "Let's go for a little ride."

We hopped into the blue 1969 Mustang which had been prepared for the flying start mile and kilometer speed runs. Mickey strapped himself in and put on his helmet while I crouched on the floor hanging on to the roll cage tubing. "What am I doing here?" I thought. Mickey then took me on a high-speed trip up and down the course at 150 mph, showing me how to spot soft salt and other speed killers.

"Thanks, Joe," I shouted afterwards while climbing out through the window, "I think!"

As it turned out, most of Joe's USAC crew were his racing buddies from the Thirties, now retired from various careers. They killed time telling funny stories (gallows humor mostly) of their exploits riding motorcycles on dirt and board tracks. Joe mentioned that he had ridden Excelsior Motorcycles (from 1926 through 1931) before he landed finally with Harley-Davidson. At Excelsior, Joe both raced and designed the machines. Excelsior was owned by Schwinn Bicycle Company in Chicago and run by Ignaz Schwinn.

Back in the beginning days of the Great Depression, Excelsior wanted to create a performance image in Europe by racing in the major motorcycle classics. Ignaz Schwinn assembled a team of riders and mechanics with a full complement of racing motorcycles and shipped them off to the continent. The young racers took advantage of the situation, and lack of supervision, by partying heartily through the season with commensurate poor racing results on the tracks. By season's end they had exhausted their funds, and Schwinn's patience, and wanted to return home. Since they had earlier sold their return boat tickets to support their profligate lifestyle, they wired Excelsior for more money to book passage. They received a two-word telegram in response: "SWIM! SCHWINN!" The Depression took Excelsior

Joe Petrali at Harley-Davidson

down with it in 1931. Petrali was promptly called up to Milwaukee, and signed with Harley-Davidson.

While I knew Joe was a motorcycle racer in the pre-war era, it was much later I learned of his great career. He had shown me his American Motorcyclist Association (AMA) membership card (No. 1) on one occasion. Joe was the AMA national board track champion in 1925. He also was the AMA national dirt track champion five times (!) between 1931 and 1936. Even more amazing, he was AMA national hill climb champion eight times (!!). During that run of hill climbs he won 31 climbs in a row – starting on the first climb attempt! His dirt track domination included 25 dirt track nationals victories in two years, 12 in one year and all 13 in another. To top it all off, he set the world motorcycle speed record on March 13, 1937 on Daytona Beach, Florida, at 136.183 mph on a streamlined Harley-Davidson.

Joe Petrali and his motorcycle land speed record
Harley-Davidson

In 1938 he walked away from motorcycle racing for good (at least as a competitor) and began his career in aviation, first at Douglas Aircraft, followed by the Hughes Aircraft Company. And the rest, as the saying goes, is history.

Today, Joe's lasting influence on Harley-Davidson heritage can be witnessed at the Harley-Davidson Museum in Milwaukee. In the Competition Gallery, where there is a reproduction of a Twenties-vintage board track with 45-degree banking, four of Joe's H-D racing bikes are on display, including the Daytona world record breaker.

And his echo still reverberates in land speed racing via his photographer son Dave, who was a member of the timing team for *The Blue Flame* at Bonneville in 1970 and then took over his father's role as chief timer on the successful world land speed record attempts of Richard Noble and Andy Green, including

Gary and Joe Petrali discussing the USAC/FIA timing

their remarkable supersonic triumph in 1997, and is a member of the FIA Land Speed Records Commission.

Gary getting the good news from Joe Petrali that he is the new world land speed record holder – fastest man on the Earth

AFTERWORD

The Record

Gary Gabelich and *The Blue Flame* held the World Land Speed Record at 630.388 mph, set over the kilometer, for 13 years. Englishman Richard Noble, after an unsuccessful attempt at Bonneville in 1981 and another at Black Rock Desert in Nevada in 1982, finally drove his Rolls-Royce turbojet-powered *Thrust2* to a new World Land Speed Record of 633.468 mph through the mile at Black Rock on October 4, 1983. Noble's 634.051 mph through the kilometer, however, was insufficient to better our kilometer figure by the FIA-mandated 1%. Our kilometer record would thus remain intact, though no longer fast enough to count as the Absolute World Land Speed Record, for 27 years, until Andy Green's spectacular 713.990 mph run in *ThrustSSC* on September 25, 1997. He subsequently raised his own records again to 763.305 mph through the mile and 760.303 mph through the kilometer during his historic supersonic milestone runs on October 15.

The Car

When Reaction Dynamics failed to make its land speed record attempt in 1969, ownership of *The Blue Flame* devolved to the Institute of Gas Technology as per contractual agreement. After Gary broke Craig Breedlove's record, the American Gas Association exhibited the car across the United States throughout 1971, at numerous automobile and natural gas industry trade shows and the Indianapolis 500 opening ceremonies. Then, it was off to Europe in the care of Gerard Brennan. Finally, *The Blue Flame* was sold and shipped back to Europe. Initially, it was kept in a private museum in Belgium. Now, after another change of ownership, it has become the feature attraction at the Auto und Technik Museum in Sinsheim, Germany, not far from the Hockenheim race track, where it remains hugely popular as the first World Land Speed Record breaker to exceed 1000 kph.

The Driver

In the immediate aftermath of his record-breaking run, Gary Gabelich was whisked off to New York to appear on several network television talk shows, such as Johnny Carson and the Today Show, and toured the world as a spokesperson for the American Natural Gas Industry. Later, he was selected for a USO tour to Viet Nam and helped to entertain the US troops.

Eventually he resumed drag racing on land and water. He had a serious accident in his new exhibition Funny Car, in which he almost lost both legs and an arm. But amazingly he was able to recover fully, and also to shrug off the effects of a crash in a drag boat at Turlock Lake in 1975.

In 1983 he visited the *Thrust2* team at Black Rock Desert, where he outlined plans for a *The Blue Flame*-like rocket car called The *American Way,* but sadly while riding his beloved Harley-Davidson motorcycle to the Long Beach seashore in January, 1984, he was hit by a truck and killed.

A Long Beach city park was dedicated to his memory in 1985.

The Reactions Dynamics LSR Team

Understandably, overshadowed by the notoriety accorded to Gary Gabelich and the Natural Gas Industry's publicity campaign, the real story about the Reaction Dynamics land speed record team remained untold until now.

Ray Dausman, Pete Farnsworth and I created a new paradigm in automobile racing with the introduction of controllable rocket propulsion in the *X-1* and then *The Blue Flame*.

We designed and built from scratch the entire land speed record (LSR) vehicle, *The Blue Flame*. Scaled up from the original 25-lb thrust prototype engine and designed for a land speed record attempt exclusively, the Reaction Dynamics 22,000 lb thrust rocket propulsion system for the LSR vehicle was our third in a series of rocket designs. *The Blue Flame*'s chassis was a unique aircraft-style riveted monocoque construction. Even the forged aluminum wheels were a custom design.

On our first-ever attempt to set the World Land Speed Record we successfully raised the mark by 30 mph! This was accomplished with the rocket motor de-tuned to almost one-half of its full power, complying with the 700 mph speed restrictions imposed by tire supplier, Goodyear Tire & Rubber Company.

The Blue Flame still retains the World Records for the kilometer and mile in the FIA Category C: Rocket Class. USAC Chief Steward Joe Petrali related that it was the first (and only) American World Land Speed Record contender to capture the record on its first venture to the Bonneville Salt Flats.

As you can read elsewhere in this book, I went on to build more rockets. Pete went back to building automobile transporters. After leaving us to work for a Milwaukee engineering company, Ray eventually worked in waste water treatment facility design and maintenance.

While the three of us had originally designed *The Blue Flame* ultimately to break the sound barrier on land, intending to do so the following year, that never happened. First of all, the desire to get the supersonic record was ours, not the Institute of Gas Technology's. Second, the car was stripped of all the fuel tanks and other accoutrements, hoses, lines, controls, etc., so that it could go on its world tour and generate maximum publicity. It couldn't run again without a major rebuild, which included adding the full-size LNG tank and rebuilding the rocket motor to run the higher LNG flow rate. Finally, IGT believed there was no upside, only a possible downside, to running the car once more and deemed that it would never race again.

The Bonneville Salt Flats

The Blue Flame was the last vehicle to establish the World's Land Speed Record on the famed Bonneville Salt Flats in Utah.

ACKNOWLEDGMENTS

C. Thomas Sylke, attorney at law provided much help with intellectual property issues.

Gerard Brennan whose memory for detail is extraordinary.

Howard Carpenter had some great recollections of his time with Chuck Suba.

Tom Daniel, a partner of Gary Gabelich in Rocketman Productions, knew Gary's post-record challenges.

Dean Dietrich kept the land speed record project viable with his careful business management as budgets and schedules continually extended.

Don Edwards

Don Garlits is a great friend and storyteller.

Bob Kachler

Art Malone had more input on Suba's jet car fixation.

Tom "Mongoose" McEwen grew up with Gary and shared his experiences in the old neighborhood.

Jean Ann (Suba) Medd still looks up to her late big brother.

Dr. Tom Morel translated Paul Torda's ideas into action.

David Petrali keeps his father's legend alive and still times world land speed records.

Dr. Bob Rosenberg was they key early enthusiast in the natural gas industry that really made the project possible.

Jake Schuljak partnered with Chuck Suba and supported his ambition to be the fastest in the world.

Gary Scow was Gabelich's 'wing man' in drag racing and boat racing.

Bob Stange and Edgar Stoffels were successful race car builders in Suba's 'Evanston Mafia'.

Kerrie Supanich is West Wendover's public face.

Dr. S. Carl Uzgiris provided amazing support from IIT.

Alan Visovatti had many memories to share of Chuck Suba.

Don Waldschmidt shared his comprehensive archive of Gary Gabelich.

APPENDICES

Appendix I
X-1 TIMELINES

September 2, 1963

Ray watches first drag race at NHRA Indy Nationals

Summer, 1964

HPR-25 tests – Ray Dausman and Dick Keller test their 25 pound thrust hydrogen peroxide monopropellant rocket using a bathroom scale and movie camera to record performance in Blue Island, IL behind Ray Muller's home.

September, 1964

Dick recognizes Pete Farnsworth at Oswego, IL drag strip and discusses the rocket dragster concept

October, 1964

Ray and Dick discuss HPR-25 test results and concept for a rocket dragster at Pete's home in Milwaukee, Pete agrees to join project, moving on to phase two of the LSR program

January, 1965

Dick writes first LSR proposal, "Development of a Land Speed Record Vehicle of Mach One Capability" to promote sponsor support and to help promote the three phase project to break the land speed record and the sound barrier

March, 1965

IITRI Spectra (IIT Research Institute monthly publication) announces the rocket dragster project, "A Dragster's Dream"

Spring, 1965

Work begins on the *X-1* rocket and chassis

June, 1965

HPR-2500 hydrogen peroxide rocket motor (built at IIT Research Institute) finished and project first mentioned in *Drag World, "Rocket Car Planned",* report by Ben Brown

April, 1966

Dick begins work at IGT as Chief Technologist, Gas Reaction Kinetics Research

July 23, 1966

X-1 tests at Great Lakes Dragaway-

Dick drives *X-1* in two static tests in the shut off area alongside the track, then two runs on the drag strip.

One objective was to show the *X-1* rocket control by staging on the drag strip, then two short runs with 2 second burns to 70 or 80 mph; no parachutes were on the car.

August, 1966

Dick meets with Chuck Suba to propose driving the *X-1*

September 6, 1966

Chuck drives *X-1* in first full ¼-mile tests at Great Lakes Dragaway

7.19 seconds ET at 203.39 miles per hour, mentioned in *Drag World* report by Ben Brown

Fall, 1966

Ray moves to Milwaukee to work at Allis-Chalmers on fuel cell technology

April, 1967

Pete finishes *X-1* bodywork, *X-1* ready to run fully completed

1967 X-1 Drag Race Results

Venue	Date	E.T., sec	Speed, mph
Rockford, IL	08/13/67	6.30	200.000
Crown Point, IN	08/20/67	6.57	160.714
		6.41*	189.470
Union Grove, WI	09/02/67	7.06	152.520
		6.78	229.290
	09/03/67	6.42	214.280
		6.52	196.720
Rockford, IL	09/04/67	6.32	193.000
Alton, IL	09/10/67	6.77	174.000
		6.70	198.000
Cincinnati, OH	09/24/67	6.77	156.520
		6.53	170.770
Union Grove, WI	10/22/67	6.44	210.520

*Note: ET was given as 5.41 seconds, but not considered credible by Reaction Dynamics

February, 1968

Dick writes new LSR project proposal to gas industry, *"LNG Goes Supersonic"*

April, 1968

Dick revises LSR project proposal to the gas industry, *"Setting the New World Land Speed Record with LNG Fuel"*

1968 X-1 Drag Race Results

Venue	Date	E.T., sec	Speed, mph
Oswego, IL	05/26/68	6.28	214.280
		6.03	257.140
Rockford, IL	07/06/68	6.216	251.390
		6.072	248.610
Oklahoma City, OK	09/15/68	6.09	257.880
		5.90	265.480

October 13, 1968

Chuck Suba killed in Fuel Dragster crash at Rockford Dragway in Byron, IL

RICHARD KELLER & DAVID TREMAYNE

Appendix II
Initial LSR Project Correspondence

July 20, 1967

Contacted Ted Hollingsworth at STP Corporation in Des Plaines, IL with LSR proposal.

July 26, 1967

Dr. Henry Linden, director of the Institute of Gas Technology (IGT) at IIT, wrote to Chet Stackpole, American Gas Association (AGA) managing director, advising support for a land speed record (LSR) project and requesting sponsor support from the members of **$124,000**.

August 10, 1967

Contacted William McCrary, manager of race tire development at Firestone Tire and Rubber Company regarding LSR tires for the project. Firestone had supplied tires and was kept in the loop during the *X-1* project. Following Art Arfons high speed crash in 1966 at Bonneville, a decision was made to discontinue LSR support.

November 27, 1967

Clark Daugherty, president, Rockwell Manufacturing Company, responded to Dr. Henry Linden's memorandum that he saw the potential benefit of the LSR project.

November 30, 1967

Jack Tankersley, president of East Ohio Gas Company, wrote Dr. Henry Linden questioning whether any tire company had been contacted by Reaction Dynamics.

December 26, 1967

Jim Condon, executive vice president of Peoples Gas Light and Coke Company wrote Dr. Henry Linden with opinion that the project was too dangerous.

December 27, 1967

Bill Strauss, chairman and president, Northern Natural Gas Company, Omaha, wrote to Dr. Henry Linden that not much industry technical knowledge would be gained by supporting the project.

February 28, 1968

Dick Keller wrote Dr. Robert Rosenberg, manager of utilization research at IGT, that there had been discussions with Jerry Tiffin, product manager, race tire group, Goodyear Tire and Rubber Company. He proposed a meeting with the race tire sales and engineering group as well as the aerospace division to discuss possible areas of sponsorship. Those included:

- Race car tires for the LSR attempt
- Lightweight alloy wheels
- Disk brake system
- Costs of timing and course preparation

- Lightweight pressurized cryogenic LNG tank
- Lightweight pressure vessels
- Drag parachutes
- Supersonic braking system

April 8, 1968

Marvin Chandler, chairman and president, Northern Illinois Gas sent proposal to 40 natural gas distributors, 5 pipeline companies, and 3 gas industry suppliers, requesting project support for **$200,000**.

May 6, 1968

Dr. Robert Rosenberg wrote Henry Harper, vice president of public relations, Northern Illinois Gas, discussing positive safety argument for the project.

June 7, 1968

Dr. Robert Rosenberg wrote Harold Walker, director of public affairs, AGA, discussing safety and publicity benefits of the project.

July 10, 1968

Buell Duncan, president, American Gas Association, to cooperate with Henry Harper and Northern Illinois Gas in solicitation of project support of **$225,000**.

July 30, 1968

Jack Reid, associate director at IGT wrote to Pete Farnsworth of Reaction Dynamics authorizing initial expenditure up to $50,000 to launch project and cover expenses until December 31, 1968. *The Blue Flame* project begins.

Attached was a project timeframe **estimated at a budget of $147,000** with record attempts in September through October 1969.

Appendix III

Reaction Dynamics progress reports to IGT from August, 1968 through November, 1969

August, 1968

The project began

Shop in Milwaukee was rented at 5254 N.124th Street

Dr. T. Paul Torda, associate professor of Mechanical and Aerospace Engineering at Illinois Institute of Technology (IIT) agreed to consult on the aerodynamics design and overall vehicle performance.

Tom Morel, a graduate student under Dr. Torda, begins working on his master's thesis research.

September, 1968

The *X-1* was prepared for the Oklahoma City jet car race – executives from Northern Illinois Gas, American Gas Association, and Institute of Gas Technology to attend

An agreement was signed with James McCormick of FMC Inorganic Chemicals Division to consult with Ray Dausman on the bipropellant propulsion system design.

The Bonneville international course was surveyed to provide data for the vehicle suspension design.

Dr. S. Carl Uzgiris, assistant professor of Mechanical and Aerospace Engineering at IIT agreed to consult on the structural design of the vehicle and recruit engineering master's degree candidates for thesis research.

October, 1968

Chuck Suba, driver designate of *The Blue Flame*, was killed in a drag racing accident in a fuel dragster at the Rockford, Illinois drag strip.

A driver replacement search was initiated. Five finalists were selected for interviewing after reviewing numerous resumes. The list included Don Garlits, Don Beeman, Doug Rose, Craig Breedlove, and Chris Karamesines. Experience in high speed race cars and name recognition were considerations at this time.

Goodyear declined to provide any support beyond tires. The tire they will supply is the 8.00-25 LSR tire used on the front of Breedlove's Sonic 1 record-setter. It is 35 inches in OD. These are much larger than the Firestone 7.00-18, 28 inch OD tires that the vehicle design has been modeled to use. A search for a wheel supplier was begun.

The Ohio State University (OSU) transonic wind tunnel facility was contacted to provide data for the vehicle design.

A 1/5 scale model of *The Blue Flame* was built to use for PR appearances.

The propulsion system design was begun at Engineering Design Service Company in Buffalo, New York with Jim McCormick.

November, 1968

After interviewing the driver candidates, Don Garlits agreed to drive The Blue Flame.

Dr. John D. Lee at OSU agreed to work with Dr. Torda and Tom Morel testing the land speed record vehicle design.

The propulsion system design is nearing completion and final construction cost quotation.

Dr. Uzgiris recruited five additional graduate students to begin work on the vehicle structural design; Messrs. Adhikari, Desai, Kurani, Parikh, and Thakur.

December, 1968

No report.

The AGA and IGT agreed to underwrite the **continuation of the LSR project to $147,000**. Gary Gabelich visited Reaction Dynamics to propose driving the *X-1* rocket dragster. Since the car was retired, Gary left without a deal.

January, 1969

OSU tunnel testing has begun. Vehicle performance calculations were completed, driving the propulsion system final design and vehicle design.

Goodyear has required the tires not be run at speeds in excess of 700 mph for the first attempts at the land speed record.

In order to assure *The Blue flame* will stay within the speed cap, the rocket system has been configured to operate at a down-rated maximum thrust for the lower speed runs.

The vehicle wheel design and structural design drawings will begin to be available next month.

A quote for the rocket motor assembly has been firmed at $27,000. The whole propulsion system will now cost $79,000.

February, 1969

A permit for a record attempt in September, 1969 was cleared by Joe Petrali at United States Auto Club (USAC), the Bonneville Speedway Association, and ACCUS-FIA.

Reaction Dynamics, Inc. was registered as the USAC car owner of record.

Naming a reserve driver was contemplated in the event the driver designate was not available at the time of the record attempt.

Fabricating techniques, equipment and fixtures were developed at Reaction Dynamics.

OSU transonic wind tunnel work was completed. An un-faired rear strut design was selected based upon the OSU data, eliminating the wheel fairings and wing-like struts.

The 22,000 pound thrust rocket propulsion system fabrication was begun, delivery expected in May.

The hydrogen peroxide propellant tank was designed for fabrication.

A 750 mph wheel design was completed. This aluminum wheel is for the initial subsonic runs and may be replaced by a higher speed wheel later for supersonic record attempts.

March, 1969

The chassis jig was erected for assembly of the vehicle. A dimpling press was fabricated to prepare the skin panels for riveting.

Parachute canisters (3 pairs) were fabricated and shipped to Deist Safety Equipment for final assembly.

A construction and test calendar was revised.

April, 1969

The press kit was assembled for the AGA press conference at the Beverly Hills Hotel in California with Jim Chatfield. *The Blue Flame* LSR project was announced to the world.

Dr. Uzgiris evaluated possible instrumentation requirements and contacted NASA for an equipment loan.

The plumbing design layout was completed. The rocket assembly is now due for shipment in June instead of May.

Two additional mechanics were hired for fabrication in the shop.

Welding fixtures for the aluminum rings (ribs) were built and tested.

May, 1969

No report.

Don Garlits decided against driving just prior to the AGA press conference. Gary Gabelich was contacted and interviewed for the LSR driver position after the press conference.

June, 1969

The propulsion system control mechanism design was completed. It consists of a fluidic (air) binary pneumatic logic circuit.

LNG fuel lines are behind schedule.

The high-pressure titanium nitrogen spheres are behind schedule.

The rocket assembly and hydrogen peroxide tank are now scheduled for July delivery.

The chassis central monocoque structure being assembled on the chassis fixture is nearing completion.

Aluminum forgings have been completed for the wheels and shipped to Cragar in California for final machining.

Gary Gabelich signed the driver agreement. A reserve driver will be named as well.

July, 1969

The rocket motor assembly arrived. After inspection, it was returned to the fabricator for necessary modifications. It is expected to be returned to Reaction Dynamics in August.

The hydrogen peroxide tank has arrived and all pressurized systems have been tested.

The Cragar wheels are in the machining process. The wheels will be assembled at Reaction Dynamics, and then sent to Goodyear for tire mounting, balancing, and testing.

Parachutes are due from Deist in August.

The aluminum LSR vehicle trailer is under construction.

August, 1969

The rocket motor modifications are completed and the motor will be returned in September.

The completed fuel system has been tested and calibrated.

The monocoque chassis has been rotated upright on the assembly fixture for final assembly.

The first wheels have arrived from Cragar and prepared to transport to Goodyear in Akron, Ohio.

September, 1969

The complete propulsion system is ready to install in the chassis.

The monocoque hatch covers are nearing completion.

The front suspension and steering assemblies are being fabricated.

Formed aluminum rear body panels are ready for mounting.

The formed aluminum cockpit canopy is being fabricated.

The vertical stabilizer assembly is being fabricated in a fixture.

Twelve wheels were assembled and taken to Goodyear for balancing and dynamic testing.

The vehicle trailer is being assembled.

October, 1969

No report.

November, 1969

Ray Dausman left Reaction Dynamics and the LSR project

No report.

1970 Events

Car taken from Reaction Dynamics to Illinois

Returned to RDI in Wisconsin for completion

Southern Gas Association appearance to promote funding at Houston Astroworld Park

Final static testing at Union Grove week of July 27, 1970

September 12, 1970

Reaction Dynamics crew and *The Blue Flame* leave Milwaukee shop and caravan to the Bonneville Salt Flats

Appendix IV. USAC/FIA Log Book 09/14/1970 – 10/23/1970

						USAC/FIA LOG BOOK – THE BLUE FLAME AT BONNEVILLE
						Existing World Land Speed Record is 600.601mph - must exceed 606.607mph (101% of LSR) to break the record
DATE	RUN	DISTANCE	TIME	MPH	DIRECTION	NOTES
9/14/2007						team arrives on salt
9/15/1970						changing wheel bearings - set up pits
9/16/1970						vehicle preparations
9/17/1970	1	SS 1/4-mile	10.517	85.576	north	average speed for distance - standing start
9/18/1970	2	SS 1/4-mile	9.851	91.360	north	average speed for distance - standing start
	3	SS 1/4-mile	6.724	133.849	south	average speed for distance - standing start
	3	SS 500 meters	7.844	142.589	south	average speed for distance - standing start
9/19/1970	4	Mile	21.261	169.324	north	mile 4 to 5 - test run
	4	Mile	9.461	380.509	north	mile 5 to 6 - test run
	4	Kilometer	5.603	399.240	north	mile 5 to 6 - test run
	4	2000 feet trap	3.858	353.309	north	reference data only
9/20/1970						no runs - publicity photos
9/21/1970	5	Mile	11.094	324.499	north	mile 4 to 5 - 1st test run
	5	Mile	8.449	426.085	north	mile 5 to 6 - 1st test run
	5	Kilometer	5.203	429.931	north	mile 5 to 6 - 1st test run
	5	2000 feet trap	3.246	419.922	north	mile 5 to 6 - 1st test run - reference data only
	6	Mile	10.810	333.025	north	mile 4 to 5 - 2nd test run
	6	Mile	8.530	422.039	north	mile 5 to 6 - 2nd test run
	6	Kilometer	5.267	424.707	north	mile 5 to 6 - 2nd test run

Date	No.	Unit	Value 1	Value 2	Direction	Comment
9/22/1970	6	2000 feet trap	3.263	417.735	north	mile 5 to 6 - 2nd test run - reference data only
9/23/1970						rocket motor repairs
						rocket motor repairs
9/24/1970						rocket motor reassembled after crack repaired
9/25/1970	7	Mile	10.453	344.398	north	test run - H2O2 only
	7	Kilometer	6.803	328.815	north	
	7	2000 feet trap	3.650	373.443	north	
9/26/1970						Dick Keller returns to Milwaukee to fabricate replacement H2O2 catalyst pack
9/27/1970						
9/28/1970						
9/29/1970						
9/30/1970						
10/1/1970						
10/2/1970						
10/3/1970						
10/4/1970						
10/5/1970						
10/6/1970						The Blue Flame rocket motor is repaired and returned to course
10/7/1970						no runs - high winds
10/8/1970						no runs - high winds
10/9/1970	8	mile	8.768	410.584	north	
	8	kilometer	5.823	384.150	north	
	8	2000 feet trap	2.945	462.840	north	reference data only
	9	mile	7.678	468.872	south	
	9	kilometer	4.829	463.230	south	
	9	2000 feet trap	2.849	478.440	south	reference data only
10/10/1970						no runs - high winds

Date	No.	Distance	Time	Speed	Direction	Notes
10/11/1970	10	mile	7.435	484.196	south	H2O2 only - test run
	10	kilometer	4.539	492.824	south	
	10	2000 feet trap	2.896	470.672	south	reference data only
	11	mile	7.544	477.200	north	H2O2 and LNG
	11	kilometer	4.804	465.639	north	
	11	2000 feet trap	2.740	497.470	north	reference data only
	12	mile	6.462	557.103	south	
	12	kilometer	4.020	556.451	south	
	12	2000 feet trap	2.442	558.177	south	reference data only
	13	mile	6.484	555.212	north	parachute failure - went into mud at mile 13
	13	kilometer	4.064	550.426	north	
10/12/1970						cleaning car from mud and salt
10/13/1970	14	mile	6.619	543.889	north	parachute test
	14	kilometer	4.156	538.241	north	
	14	2000 feet trap	2.463	553.418	north	reference data only
10/14/1970						installed push bar to save fuel on acceleration - no runs - high winds
10/15/1970	15	mile	6.586	546.614	north	
	15	kilometer	4.077	548.671	north	
	15	2000 feet trap	2.509	543.271	north	reference data only
	16	mile	6.358	566.216	south	
	16	kilometer	3.850	581.021	south	
	16	2000 feet trap	2.508	543.488	south	reference data only
	17	mile	5.911	609.034	south	
	17	kilometer	3.670	609.518	south	H2O2 leak - couldn't make return run
10/16/1970						no runs - rocket motor calibration (tuning)
10/17/1970						no runs - rocket motor calibration (tuning)
10/18/1970	18	mile	no time		north	unable to complete north run due to check valve malfunction

Date	Marker	Unit	Time	Speed	Direction	Notes
	19	mile	5.791	621.654	south	mile record try outbound run
	19	kilometer	3.603	620.853	south	kilo record try outbound run
	20	mile	5.960	604.027	north	mile record try return run - 601.655 / average
	20	kilometer	3.736	598.750	north	kilo record try return run - 603.760 / average
	21	mile	6.007	599.300	south	
	21	kilometer	3.674	608.855	south	
10/19/1970						waiting for LNG and 98% H_2O_2
10/20/1970						waiting for LNG and 98% H_2O_2
10/21/1970						LNG and 98% H_2O_2 arrive for final attempts
10/22/1970						no runs - high winds
	22	mile	no time		north	warmup run on H_2O_2 only
10/23/1970	23	mile	5.829	617.602	south	mile record try outbound run
10/23/1970	23	kilometer	3.543	631.367	south	kilo record try outbound run
	24	mile	5.739	627.287	north	mile record try return run - 622.407 / average
	24	kilometer	3.554	629.412	north	kilo record try return run - 630.388 / average
				SNOW BEGINS		

The world record course laid out by USAC for FIA records is 10 miles in length with a mile marker at each mile. Record runs are typically timed between miles 5 and 6 northbound. The kilometer speed trap begins 2,000 feet north of the mile 5 marker and ends coincident with mile 6. Data collected over the 2,000 feet distance and the kilometer distance (3280 feet) were used to analyze the optimal performance of The Blue Flame, as it was intended to accelerate under power into the measured mile and cease power (run out of fuel) at the midpoint, coasting out of the mile.

USAC-FIA timing crew were: Joe Petrali, Ben Torres, Glen Bjorklund, and David Petrali

BIBLIOGRAPHY

References

Keller, R., "LNG Goes Supersonic", Proposal No. U7S2/68A, Institute of Gas Technology, IIT Center, Chicago, Illinois, Feb. 1968

Adhikari, M.C., "Design of the 'Blue Flame' Vehicle – Structure", M.M.E. Report, Department of Aerospace and Mechanical Engineering, Illinois Institute of Technology, Oct. 1969.

Desai, K.C., "Design of the 'Blue Flame' Vehicle – Connectors", M.M.E. Report, Department of Aerospace and Mechanical Engineering, Illinois Institute of Technology, Dec. 1970.

Kurani, S.V., "Structural Design of an LSR Vehicle", MS thesis, Department of Aerospace and Mechanical Engineering, Illinois Institute of Technology, Dec. 1969.

Morel, T.A., "Aerodynamic Design of a High Speed Rocket Car", MS thesis, Department of Aerospace and Mechanical Engineering, Illinois Institute of Technology, June 1969.

Parikh, H., "Design of the 'Blue Flame' Vehicle – Wheels", M.M.E. Report, Department of Aerospace and Mechanical Engineering, Illinois Institute of Technology, Jan. 1970.

Thakur, P.T., "Design of the 'Blue Flame' Vehicle – Suspension", M.M.E. Report, Department of Aerospace and Mechanical Engineering, Illinois Institute of Technology, Jan. 1970.

Uzgiris, S.C. and Pandey, K.G., "Performance of the 'Blue Flame", unpublished report, Mar. 1970.

Torda, T.P. and Morel, T.A., "Aerodynamic Design of a Land Speed Record Car", *J. Aircraft*, vol. 8, no. 12, Dec. 1971, pp. 1029-1033.

SOURCE OF ILLUSTRATIONS

The authors would like to thank the following people and organizations who have kindly supplied photographs and drawings which appear in this book:

American Gas Association, Inc.

Institute of Gas Technology

Illinois Institute of Technology

Pete and Leah Farnsworth

David Petrali

Harley-Davidson Motor Company Museum

STERN Magazine

Ohio State University

George Callaway

Gerard Brennan

Alan Visovatti

Ruth Ann Nelson

Jean Ann (Suba) Medd

Jake Schuljak

University of Utah Library

Table 1

THE BLUE FLAME PROJECT
LAND SPEED RECORD ATTEMPT - CONTRIBUTORS

Reaction Dynamics, Inc.
Land Speed Record Team

Ray Dausman

Pete Farnsworth

Dick Keller

Ken McCarth

Gerard Brennan
(alternate driver)

Dave Bykowski

Larry Henkel

Mark Neubauer

Gary Gabelich (driver of
The Blue Flame)

Reaction Dynamics, Inc.
Fabrication Team

Chuck Suba, Sr.

Ray Besasie, Sr.

Dick Huebschen

Roger Buetow

Dix Erickson

Harry Gunderson

Fred Butze

Larry Tanner

Doug Bandl

IIT Research Institute

Dr. Wilson Whaley

Allan Gaynor

Dr. Robert Bonthron

Noel Shaw

Dave Anthes

Illinois Institute of Technology

Dr. T. Paul Torda

Tom Morel

Dr. S. Carl Uzgiris

Monoj Adhikari

Shashi Kurani

Krishna Pandey

Harshad Parikh

Prahlad Thakur

Kirit Desai

The Ohio State University

Dr. John Lee

Dr. Gerald Gregorek

Institute of Gas Technology

Dr. Robert Rosenberg

Dr. Henry Linden

Institute of Gas Technology Bonneville Team

Dean Dietrich

Don Fleming

Pete Buzane

Tony Mikulic

American Gas Association and Affiliates

Hank Harper (NIGAS)

Marvin Chandler (NIGAS)

Consultant/Contractors

Jim Deist (Deist Safety Equipment Co.)

James C. McCormick (BECCO Chemical Division, FMC Corporation)

Goodyear Tire Company Bonneville Team

Mike Hopkins

Dick Ralstin

United States Auto Club (USAC)

Joe Petrali

David Petrali

L.T. "Ben" Torres

Glen R. Bjorklund

Jess Toby

Table 2

THE BLUE FLAME PROJECT
LAND SPEED RECORD ATTEMPT - CORPORATE SUPPORTERS

Aeroquip Corp., Marman Division

Cermatec Industries, Inc.

Champion spark Plug Company

Cragar Industries

E.F. Johnson Company

Goodyear Tire & Rubber Company

International Harvester Company

Jamesbury Corporation

Kelsey Hayes Company, H-H Products Division

Marotta Scientific Controls, Inc.

Micro Industries

Monroe Auto Equipment Company

Motorola Inc., Automotive Products Division

National Aeronautics and Space Administration (NASA)

PROTO Tool Company

RIX Industries

San Diego Gas and Electric Company

Snap-Tite, Inc.

The ARO Corporation

The Goodyear Tire and Rubber Company

The Timken Roller Bearing Company

Transport Dynamics, Inc.

Universal Oil Products Company, Flexonics Division

USM Corporation, USM Fastener Division

FMC Corporation

Table 3.
THE BLUE FLAME PROJECT
LAND SPEED RECORD ATTEMPT - NATURAL GAS INDUSTRY SPONSORS

The American Gas
Association (AGA)

Northern Illinois Gas
Company (NIGAS)

Institute of Gas
Technology

Alabama Gas
Corporation

Algonquin Gas
Transmission Co.

American Meter Co.

Atlanta Gas Light Co.

Baltimore Gas & Electric
Co.

Boston Gas Co.

California-Pacific Utilities
Co.

Central Illinois Light Co.

Central Telephone &
Utilities Corp.

Chicago Bridge & Iron
Co.

Cities Service Gas Co.

Colorado Interstate Gas
Co.

Connecticut Natural Gas
Corp.

The Consumers Gas Co.

Consumers Power Co.

The Dayton Power &
Light Co.

Elizabethtown Gas Co.

Florida Gas Co.

Florida Public Utilities
Co.

The Greenwich Gas Co.

Iowa-Illinois Gas &
Electric Co.

Kansas-Nebraska Natural
Gas Co.

Lone Star Gas Co.

Long Island Lighting Co.

Minneapolis Gas Co.

Minnesota Natural Gas
Co.

Mountain Fuel Supply Co.

Nashville Gas Co.

The Nebraska Natural
Gas Co.

New England Electric
System-Gas Cos.

Negea Service Corp.

North Central Public
Service Co.

Northern Natural Gas Company

Oklahoma Natural Gas Co.

Panhandle Eastern Pipeline Co.

Penn Fuel Gas Inc.

Piedmont Natural Gas Co.

Public Service Co. of Colorado

Southern California Gas Co.

Sprague Meter Co., Division of Textron

Tennessee Gas Transmission Co.

Texas Gas Transmission Corp.

Valley Gas Co.

Washington Gas Light Co.

The Washington Water Power Co.

Whirlpool Corp.

Wisconsin Fuel & Light Co.

Table 4.

X-1 ROCKET-POWERED DRAGSTER - PERFORMANCE RECORD

Location	Date	ET, sec.	Speed, mph
Union Grove, WI	09/05/66	7.19	203.390
Rockford, IL	08/13/67	6.30	200.000
Crown Point, IN	08/20/67	6.57	160.714
		6.41*	189.470
Union Grove, WI	09/02/67	7.06	152.520
		6.78	229.290
	09/03/67	6.42	214.280
		6.52	196.720
Rockford, IL	09/04/67	6.32	193.000
Alton, IL	09/10/67	6.77	174.000
		6.70	198.000
Cincinnati, OH	09/24/67	6.77	156.520
		6.53	170.770
Union Grove, WI	10/22/67	6.44	210.520
		6.25	215.560
Oswego, IL	05/26/68	6.28	214.280
		6.03	257.140
Rockford, IL	07/06/68	6.216	251.390
		6.072	248.610
Oklahoma City, OK	09/15/68	6.09	257.880
		5.90	265.480

*Note: Elapsed time was reported as 5.41 seconds. This seemed questionable at the time, due to either timer error or track length discrepancy. 6.41 seconds was thought to be the more accurate ET. A similar situation occurred at Oklahoma City, as the announced ETs were 1 second less.

X-1 ROCKET-POWERED DRAGSTER -
SPECIFICATIONS

NAME OF CAR:	*X-1*
CLASS:	**Unlimited Dragster**
BODY STYLE:	**Single-seat, enclosed cockpit, open-wheeled**
DRIVER:	**Charles M. (Chuck) Suba**
CAR OWNER:	**Reaction Dynamics, Inc.**
ENGINE:	**Reaction Dynamics HPR-2500, 90% hydrogen peroxide liquid monopropellant rocket**
THRUST:	**0 to 2500 pounds, continuously variable by driver**
JET HORSEPOWER:	**2800 jet horsepower at 300 mph**
ENGINE WEIGHT:	**56 pounds**
DRIVE TRAIN:	**jet-thrust driven**
THROTTLE:	**continuously variable manual control**
FUEL TANK:	**11.8 gallons stainless steel high-pressure tank**
EMPTY WEIGHT:	**720 pounds**
GROSS WEIGHT:	**980 pounds, includes driver and fuel**

CHASSIS:	steel multiple spaced tube frame with stressed panels
BODY:	aluminum skin with fiberglass nosepiece
WINDSHIELD:	3/16-inch formed Plexiglas
WHEELBASE:	120 inches
TRACK:	54.5 inch front, 58 inch rear
STEERING:	rack and pinion
SUSPENSION:	4 wheel, independently sprung, solid rear optional
TIRES:	9.50-15 Indy car (Firestone and Goodyear)
WHEELS:	Halibrand cast magnesium
BRAKES:	4 wheel disk/caliper, dual master cylinder
PARACHUTES:	two 8 feet diameter ribbon, one 16 feet diameter, emergency only
MAX ACCELERATION:	2.5 g's

Table 5

THE BLUE FLAME LAND SPEED RECORD
VEHICLE SPECIFICATIONS

NAME OF CAR:	*The Blue Flame*
RACING CLASS:	**FIA Category C - Special Vehicles**
SPONSOR:	**Natural Gas Industry of the United States**
OWNER:	**Institute of Gas Technology, Chicago, IL**
DESIGNER & BUILDER:	**Reaction Dynamics, Inc. Milwaukee, WI**
WORLD RECORD SPEED (LSR) - FLYING START KILOMETER:	**1,014.3 kilometers per hour (630.388 mile per hour)**
WORLD RECORD SPEED - FLYING START MILE:	**622.407 miles per hour (1,001.667 kilometers per hour)**
MAXIMUM SPEED DURING FASTEST RUN (EST.):	**660 miles per hour (~0.9 Mach)**
DATE:	**October 23, 1970**
LOCATION:	**Bonneville Salt Flats Wendover, UT**

RECORD SANCTIONED BY:	United States Auto Club (USAC) Indianapolis, IN
RECORD CERTIFIED BY:	Federation Internationale de la Automobile (FIA), Paris, France
DRIVER:	Gary Gabelich Long Beach, CA
REACTION DYNAMICS LSR CREW:	Pete Farnsworth Dick Keller Gerard Brennan (alt. driver) Ken McCarthy Dave Bykowski Larry Henkel Mark Neubauer
INSTITUTE OF GAS TECHNOLOGY CREW:	Dean Dietrich Don Fleming Pete Busane Tony MikuliC
AERODYNAMICS, STRUCTURAL, AND PERFORMANCE CALCULATIONS, DESIGN CONSULTING:	Illinois Institute of Technology Department of Mechanical and Aerospace Engineering Chicago, IL Dr. T. Paul Torda, professor

Tom Morel

Dr. Sarunas Carl Uzgiris, professor

Monoj Adhikari

Shashi Kurani

Harshad Parikh

Prahlad Thakur

Krishna Pandey

PREVIOUS LSR RECORD:	600.601 mph by Craig Breedlove, 1965
FIRST LSR RECORD:	39.24 mph by Count Gaston de Chasseloup-Laubat, 1898
PROJECT DESIGN GOAL:	speed of sound, Mach 1 (approx. 750 mph)
MAXIMUM DESIGN SPEED:	900-plus mph (wind tunnel tested to Mach 1.2)
ENGINE:	Reaction Dynamics HP-LNG-22000-V
ROCKET DESIGNED THRUST:	22,000 pounds maximum 16,000 pounds with first stage LNG only
MAXIMUM JET HORSEPOWER:	58,000 at 600 mph

FUEL:	**liquefied natural gas (LNG), a cryogenic liquid at minus 256 degrees Fahrenheit**
OXIDIZER:	**hydrogen peroxide, 90% concentration**
FUEL TANK:	**aluminum, insulated, pressurized by compressed helium to 500 psi**
OXIDIZER TANK:	**stainless steel, pressurized by compressed air to 500 psi**
ROCKET RUNNING TIME:	**20 seconds at full thrust**
OVERALL LENGTH:	**38 feet, 2.6 inches w/pitot tube**
OVERALL WIDTH:	**7 feet, 8 inches**
HEIGHT, TOP OF COCKPIT:	**5 feet, 1.5 inches**
HEIGHT, TOP OF STABILIZER:	**8 feet, 8 inches**
WHEELBASE:	**306.1 inches**
TRACK, FRONT:	**8.7 inches**
TRACK, REAR:	**84 inches**

WEIGHT, EMPTY:	6,500 pounds
CHASSIS:	aluminum, semi-monocoque center span; welded tubular steel structure in nose compartment and behind driver's compartment
BODY PANELS:	aluminum, stressed panels, *"POP"* riveted
SUSPENSION, FRONT:	ball-joint 4-bar link with coil/shock suspension units
SUSPENSION, REAR:	unsprung, 4130 steel tubular struts
STEERING RATIO:	90:1
TURNING RADIUS:	1/4-mile
STEERING WHEEL:	*Cragar* 3-spoke 4130 Champ Car
WHEELS:	(4) forged aluminum, 25-inch diameter, 3-piece, designed by Reaction Dynamics, built by *Cragar*

TIRES:	**8:00-25, 34.75 inches o.d., smooth tread, tubeless, 350 psi, by *Goodyear*, tested to 800-plus mph**
BRAKES:	**rear only, 14 inch diameter hard chrome faced 4340 steel disks, 2 single-piston calipers per wheel, by *H-H Products Div., Kelsey-Hayes Co.***
DRAG PARACHUTES:	**7.3 feet diameter ribbon parachute at 650 mph, 16 feet diameter ribbon at 250 mph, complete dual reserve system, by *Deist Safety Equipment***

RICHARD KELLER & DAVID TREMAYNE

Printed in Poland
by Amazon Fulfillment
Poland Sp. z o.o., Wrocław

63279490R00190